# Namibia
# Women in War

Tessa Cleaver
Marion Wallace

Foreword by Glenys Kinnock

968.81
C623

**Zed Books Ltd.**
London and New Jersey

Alverno College
Library Media Center
Milwaukee, Wisconsin

*Namibia: Women in War* was first published by Zed Books Ltd. 57 Caledonian Road, London N1 9BU, UK and 171 First Avenue, Atlantic Highlands, New Jersey 07716, USA, in 1990.

Copyright © Tessa Cleaver, Marion Wallace, 1990.

Cover designed by Sophie Buchet.
Cover photograph by Tessa Cleaver.
Typeset by EMS Photosetters, Thorpe Bay, Essex
Printed and bound in the United Kingdom
at Biddles Ltd, Guildford and King's Lynn.

All rights reserved.

**British Library Cataloguing in Publication Data**

Cleaver, Tessa
Namibia, women in war.
1. Namibia. Women. Social conditions.
I. Title II. Wallace, Marion
305.4209688

ISBN 0-86232-900-0
ISBN 0-86232-901-9 pbk

**Library of Congress Cataloging-in-Publication Data**

Cleaver, Tessa
Namibia : women in war / Tessa Cleaver,
Marion Wallace.
p. cm.
Includes bibliographical references.
ISBN 0-86232-900-0 ISBN 0-86232-901-9 (pbk.)
1. Women – Namibia – Social conditions.
2. Women, Black – Namibia. 3. National
liberation movements – Namibia.
I. Wallace, Marion. II. Title.
HQ1804.W35 1990
305.42'096881-dc20 89-48794
CIP

# Contents

# Foreword

This book clearly and unequivocally states the contribution of Namibian women to the struggle for independence and freedom. More important – the experience is conveyed through the words of the women themselves.

During my visit to Namibia in July 1989 I met many women like those who speak to us through the pages of this book. Their descriptions of their experiences, of their hopes and their fears at that time, a few months before the elections, made a deep impression on me. I recall their joy about what was happening. I recall, too, the words of a woman in Katutura who insisted that 'they must not forget us and what we did'.

I remember the old lady born in 1915, the year in which South Africa invaded German *Süd West Africa* on behalf of the British Empire. She described to me a lifetime 'spent in the dark'. She had never given up hope and had continued to support the idea that Namibia could be liberated from colonialism. She stood in line waiting to register to vote, and she told me that it was her heartfelt wish that her grandchildren would have a peaceful and secure future in a new Namibia.

When I met women in Namibia I felt optimism and joy because of their determination to make apartheid no more than a memory. They have played their part in the war against colonialism and racism and their reward should be access to real power and active participation after independence, with proper involvement at all levels of society – particularly as political representatives. The new government is committed to improving Namibian women's health, education and welfare. They must also be enabled to build up their economic strength and independence through both agriculture and industry.

Like those who speak through this book, Namibian women are not asking merely for inclusion or integration but for a central role in decision making; they have learned that. And their talents and knowledge are assets which the new democracy must use to the full.

I, like Tessa Cleaver and Marion Wallace, feel privileged to have met many women who are so remarkable, so optimistic and such resilient survivors. They have been Women in War. Now the Women in Peace must get their chance to fulfil their aspirations to help their country to emerge from the 'darkness' of conflict, inequality and grinding poverty.

**Glenys Kinnock**

# Preface

September 1989 was perhaps the most exciting and optimistic time in Namibia's history since it was colonized, but not the most convenient time to be writing a book. The picture was changing daily, as Namibia prepared itself for the first elections with democratic potential. One day witnessed the South Africans do all in their power to nullify that opportunity and the next saw with what optimism and strength the Namibian people seized it. This made clear assessments impossible. An overview of 1989 and the steps towards independence will be for others to write.

November 1989 saw elections in Namibia, observed by the UN in a country which was under the control of Pretoria: a momentous event which must have wider repercussions.

The imminent independence of Namibia was not on our agenda when we set out to gather material for the book, but stole upon us as we began to write. We continued nevertheless, because we are recording the views and stories of women as they saw things in 1988. Those stories will not be forgotten, but the mood will change, and in these pages we hope to convey something of the mood that was communicated to us then.

This book is as a result of a research visit we made from April to July 1988. The visit was set up by Church Action on Namibia with the specific aims of gathering background material for their campaigning work in order to raise awareness generally and among the churches in Britain. Information about the war and the atrocities committed by the South Africans was available in London. What we lacked was a context: the views and activities of ordinary people, and the ways in which people were managing to organize against the repression. We wanted to learn about women and women's organizations, the unions and British-based companies, the churches, and youth groups.

We set out to interview as many people as possible, with the help of translators where necessary. Initial contacts were made through the Churches, SWAPO, the unions and exiled Namibians in Britain. In August 1989, Marion paid a return visit, which enabled her to update some of the material.

Namibia, we found to be a staggeringly beautiful country – glistening mountains, deserts of dunes, wide rivers – inhabited by an optimistic and highly politicized people. The war was escalating daily, and with it the violence meted out to ordinary civilians. Tension, especially in the war zones was tangible.

People spoke cautiously and we were reliant on our friends to vouch for us and reassure those to whom we spoke that our motives were genuine. As Dr. Ihuhua at Otjimbingue said, it was a situation where: 'There are so many imposters who come here, you begin to distrust your own brother'.

Nevertheless, we were welcomed and assisted in every way possible. Hospitality and introductions were offered wherever we went, and we had the good fortune, despite transport difficulties, to travel widely, from the far north at Katima Mulilo and Ombalantu, to the south as far as Oranjemund. Time and care was freely given to fill in our lack of understanding as newcomers to the country. In return we promised to make good use of the information we received. At Engela, the women refused to tell of their experiences, because: 'We tell our stories and it only seems to get worse. The troubles here increase every day. We have told enough now . . . We are tired of telling.'

Although it has gone unrecognized, the women who talked to us run the country despite being disadvantaged. At the time of writing, it seemed they were fighting without any chances of improvement in the situation; but these chances now exist. The women are, however, well aware that the struggle on their behalf must continue.

In writing this book, we confronted the problem of how to present it in such a way that Namibian women would recognize it as reflecting the realities of their situation; how to convey their suffering as well as their strength and yet not to picture them as victims.

Another problem was how to write about a situation in which women are continually subjected to violence from men. We were anxious to avoid the possibility that we might trivialize their experience, or that by publicizing it we would be violating their privacy. As white middle-class women, we were aware of the dangers involved in writing from a point of view of privilege, relative to the women to whom we spoke; the risks of both voyeurism and profiting from others' suffering are real, and we have been concerned to ensure that we avoided both.

We hope to have achieved the right balance between giving context and not overwhelming the message of the women themselves. Awareness of the constraints our identity and our language imposed on the interviews was not lacking; some things were left unsaid and some were not easily translated.

The account does not presume to be comprehensive, nor to speak for more women than those whose words we have recorded. Our hope is to draw and maintain attention to the women's movement, as Namibian women continue to speak out. In Namibia as elsewhere, women must continue to press for justice long after liberation from South African control. And their efforts must be reciprocated and supported by their men who must take up Emma Mujoro's challenge:

> Men have no excuse. I am talking to women oppressed for years under male dominance. When are you going to work to change this? Why are [you] so slow although [you] talk of liberation?

We would like to thank all who have given us invaluable help. Space constraints prevent us acknowledging everyone individually but we would like particularly to record our gratitude to those in the Anglican church in Namibia, our colleagues here in CAN, and above all, the women in Namibia who talked to us.

*Notes*

Interviews and quotations that are not attributed were all recorded by the authors between April and July 1988. Others are from a subsequent visit made by Marion in July/August 1989.

Many of the names have been changed for reasons of security.

We have quoted prices in Rand. At the time, the exchange rate was approximately R4 to the £ sterling.

Throughout the book we have used the terms 'black', 'white' and 'coloured' for the sake of clarity. Although these are South African categorizations with which we disagree, they also reflect the class and race divisions in society in a way that cannot be ignored.

We have referred to the South African illegally appointed authorities in Namibia as a 'government' again for the sake of simplicity, although it is not recognized as such by the international community.

Tessa Cleaver and Marion Wallace

# Chronology

| | |
|---|---|
| **1884** | German occupation of Namibia |
| **1904–7** | Herero and Nama uprisings |
| **1915** | Conquest of Namibia by South Africa |
| **1917** | Rebellion of Mandume |
| **1922** | Rebellion of Bondelswarts |
| **1925** | Rebellion of Rehobothers |
| **1959** | Ovamboland People's Organization (OPO) founded<br>Forced Removal from Old Location to Katutura<br>South West Africa National Union (SWANU) founded |
| **1960** | OPO became SWAPO |
| **1964** | Odendaal Commission recommended homelands system |
| **1966** | SWAPO launched armed struggle<br>UN General Assembly ended South Africa's mandate to rule Namibia |
| **1970** | Namibia divided into 12 population groups. 'Second-tier' authorities established in following years |
| **1971** | International Court of Justice upheld decision on the mandate |
| **1971–2** | General strike |
| **1974** | Turnhalle Conference |
| **1978** | UN passed Resolution 435<br>Massacre of Namibians at Kassinga, in Angola<br>DTA formed and elected as 'government' of Namibia |
| **1986** | /Ai-//Gams Declaration |
| **1985** | Multi-Party Conference formed the Transnational Government of National Unity |
| **1988** | Defeat of South Africans at Cuito Cuanavale, Angola<br>Widespread schools boycott |
| **1989** | 1 April – Beginning of implementation of Resolution 435<br>November – Elections, won by SWAPO |
| **1990** | 21 March – independence |

# Abbreviations

| | |
|---|---|
| AG | Administrator-General |
| AMEC | African Methodist Episcopal Church |
| AWF | Anglican Women's Fellowship |
| BPWF | Business and Professional Women's Federation |
| CCN | Council of Churches in Namibia |
| CDM | Consolidated Diamond Mining |
| DRC | Dutch Reformed Church |
| DTA | Democratic Turnhalle Alliance |
| ELC | Evangelical Lutheran Church |
| ELCIN | Evangelical Lutheran Church in Namibia |
| ELOC | Evangelican Lutheran Ovambo-Kavango Church |
| ICJ | International Court of Justice |
| ILO | International Labour Organization |
| MANWU | Metal and Allied Namibian Workers' Union |
| MPLA | Popular Movement for the Liberation of Angola |
| MU | Mothers' Union |
| MUN | Mineworkers' Union of Namibia |
| NAFAU | Namibian Food and Allied Union |
| NANSO | Namibian National Students' Organization |
| NANTU | Namibian National Teachers' Union |
| NAPWU | Namibian Public Workers' Union |
| NATAU | Namibian Transport and Allied Workers' Union |
| NLP | Namibia Literacy Programme |
| NTU | Namibian Trade Union |
| NUNW | National Union of Namibian Workers |
| NWV | Namibia Women's Voice |
| OPO | Ovamboland People's Organization |
| PLAN | People's Liberation Army of Namibia |
| RMS | Rhenish Mission Society |
| SADF | South African Defence Force |
| SAPOL | South African Police |
| SWA | South West Africa |
| SWABC | South West Africa Broadcasting Corporation |
| SWANLA | South West Africa Native Labour Association |

| | |
|---|---|
| SWANU | South West Africa National Union |
| SWAPO | South West Africa People's Organisation |
| SWAPOL | South West Africa Police |
| SWATF | South West Africa Territory Force |
| SWC | SWAPO Women's Council |
| SYL | SWAPO Youth League |
| TCL | Tsumeb Corporation Ltd. |
| UNHCR | United Nations High Commission for Refugees |
| UNITA | National Union for the Total Independence of Angola |
| UNSG | United Nations Secretary General |
| UNSR | United Nations Special Representative (in Namibia) |
| UNTAG | United Nations Transition Assistance Group |
| YWCA | Young Women's Christian Association |
| 435 | United Nations Security Council Resolution No. 435 of 1978 |

Adapted from The Namibians, Minority Rights Group Report No. 19, London, 1985.

# Introduction

The year 1989 was a time of great hope for Namibia. Never had there been such an opportunity for achieving genuine independence, and Namibia's women have played a central role to bring this about.

Namibia has been a colony for more than 100 years; first ruled by Germany, and since 1915 by South Africa, its people have been subjected to a century of repression and war. In 1918, Namibia fell under the protection of the League of Nations, which delegated this authority to Britain, which in turn delegated administration of the territory to South Africa.

Britain, therefore, had a compelling responsibility to ensure that justice was done to the people of Namibia. In this it failed and must take the blame for abandoning them to terrible suffering under South African domination. Even after 1966, when South Africa's rule of Namibia was declared illegal, Britain and other Western powers continued to support the regime and to protect it from the threat of sanctions, while still profiting from the exploitation of Namibia's rich reserves of diamonds, copper and uranium.

Namibia's economy has, in fact, been geared to the needs of the territory's white minority, of South Africa and of its allies. The majority of the black population, forced to live on barren reserves, or bantustans, provided cheap labour for the whites and entered white areas only as migrant labourers. Black Namibians were driven into desperate poverty and subjected to racial discrimination and abuse. The operation of apartheid in Namibia caused at least as much suffering there as in South Africa.

But Namibians have fought against these conditions. Both the internal and exiled wings of the national liberation movement, SWAPO (South West Africa People's Organization, formed in 1960) have campaigned tirelessly for Namibia's independence. South Africa, however, consistently refused to withdraw. It was not until 1988 that military defeat in Angola and the involvement of the US and the USSR forced it to the negotiating table, where it agreed that the peace plan for Namibia passed in 1978 by the United Nations, Resolution 435, would be implemented.

The independence process that began on 1 April 1989 was designed to lead to free and fair elections on 6 November 1989. SWAPO participated in an election for the first time, and most of those forced into exile by repression and the war returned home. As we write (1989) it is not yet certain that independence will be successfully achieved. South Africa in practice retains control during the transition period and is clearly subverting the process as much as possible without actually halting it. At the time of writing, conditions for free and fair elections have not yet been established.

Despite the present uncertainty, however, considerable gains have clearly been made so far. They have been made primarily by Namibians themselves.

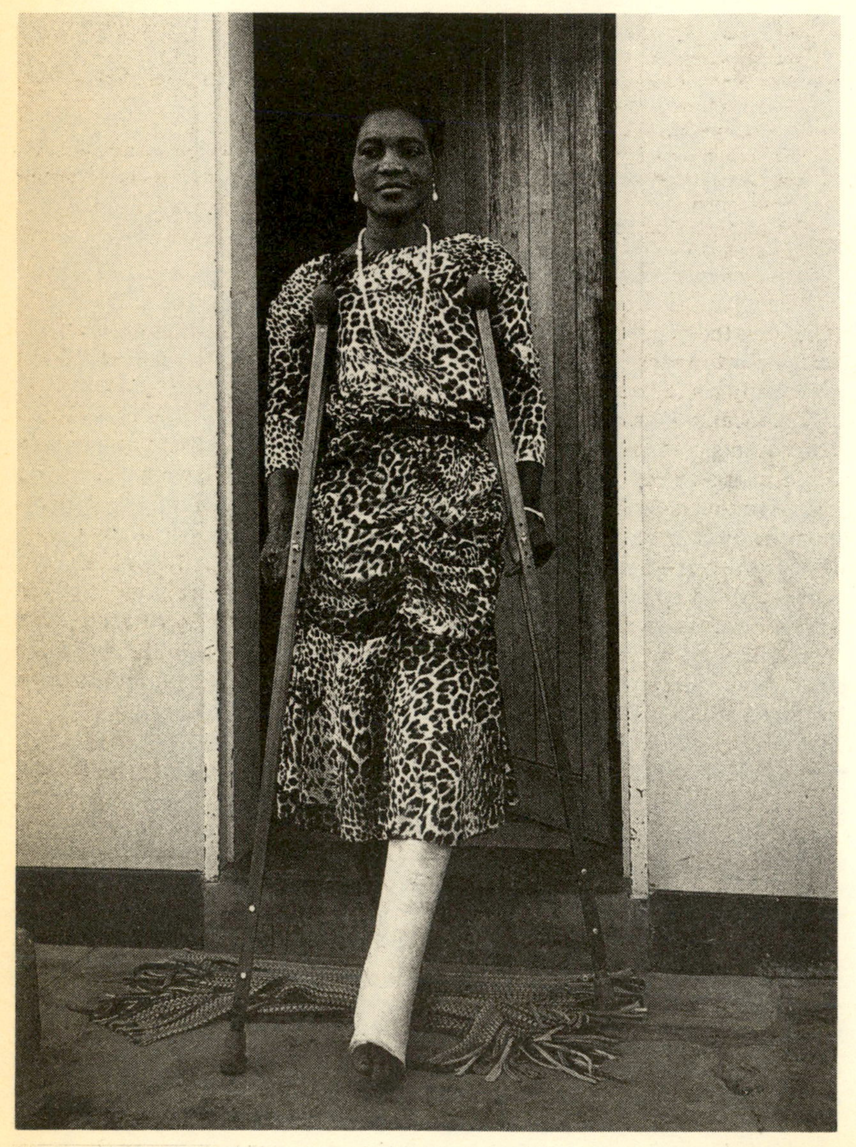

**Survivor of a bomb attack**

# 1. 'Women of Namibia are angry because of the war'

## The War

We are women in war.
We are wanting to know where help is coming from.
We are not going to tell you of our problems, because we have told our story so many times, and still no help comes.
To ask us again is like pouring petrol on fire.
We are confused. Every country sends representatives here and we tell our stories, and it only seems to get worse. The troubles here increase every day. We have told enough now.
We are tired.
We are tired of telling. Our burden is too heavy to pick up.
We are angry.
The women of Namibia are angry because of the war.

These are the words of women whose lives have been dominated by war and its effects for too long. At Engela where they live and work, violence and death were daily realities, as were constant attacks by the state 'security forces'.

The local population were perceived as the key to the survival of SWAPO combatants, and the South African forces directed much of their resources in an open policy of violent intimidation and torture of civilians. It is no exaggeration to say that this amounted to a strategy of terrorization of the local population. In the northern 'war zone', Owambo, Kavango, Caprivi and Kaoko, the population, two-thirds of which are women and children, lived under conditions of martial law. Frequent incidents of torture, rape, murder, and violent harassment have all been well documented. Under emergency legislation, Namibians may be detained indefinitely without trial; there was a strict night curfew, and people lived under the constant threat of intimidation, torture and death. Jacobina described one incident:

> In the North, I saw and heard of daily repression. For instance, a fifteen-year-old girl, Olivia Haitembu and her friend Helena Naitenge, sixteen years, were raped at Eunda by a group of Koevoet soldiers when they were returning from school in February this year [1988]. When they tried to resist their captors, they were thoroughly beaten up. Having [repeatedly] raped the children . . . the soldiers injected [them] with . . . Depo Provera. Later when the two girls were released, their buttocks swelled and they were taken to Oshandi hospital by their parents. They were discharged after two days.[1]

Incidents such as these were commonplace. Explosives are left in coke cans for children to find and detonate. Coins are left in the road to tempt them towards a buried explosive. Accusations of supporting SWAPO are accompanied by burying people's heads in the sand, beating, burning, and more. Because we are concerned to avoid giving the impression of women as victims, we shall restrict such accounts to a minimum. But it is important to record what has been happening, and the words of the women at Engela indicate the strength of will of the women behind the stories.

Reports of atrocities have been corroborated by mercenaries' statements. For example, a British mercenary in SADF's (South African Defense Force) 32 battalion said:

> Our main job is to take an area and clear it. We sweep through it and kill everything in front of us; cattle, goats, people, everything. We are out to stop SWAPO and so we stop them getting into the villages for food and water. Some of it is pretty heavy. Sometimes we take the locals for questioning. It's rough. We just beat them, cut them, burn them. As soon as we've finished with them we kill them.[2]

The repression also takes the form of kidnapping, shootings, and bombings, later blamed on SWAPO. One such case is the bombing of the First National bank at Oshakati in February 1988. Thirty-one civilians, mainly women, were killed. A survivor, Lynda, gives her account:

> When I went in the bank, I was sitting near the door. After only two minutes I heard the bomb blast . . . I couldn't see anything. I only heard people shouting 'I'm burning, I'm burning' or 'My leg is broken'. My body was just like lead. I couldn't move. I could feel that I was burning. I just decided to pray because I was going to die.

Lynda was unconscious for two weeks, suffering from first degree burns and a serious chest wound. After three weeks, it was discovered that her leg was broken.

## Women's resistance

Namibian women cannot avoid the war. They have been the object of soldiers' brutality; they have family members who are away fighting; their lives are characterized by the destitution war has brought. Most women are highly politically conscious, perceiving the war as the root of their problems. Most then choose to resist at some level.

Women's resistance to the war took on different levels: by surviving and maintaining social structures in the face of constant onslaught; by active strategies to equip themselves better for this task; by actively supporting the PLAN (People's Liberation Army of Namibia) fighters; and finally, by joining the resistance army themselves as combatants.

## Survival

Because of their socio-cultural position, women and children constituted the majority of those who remained in the villages, while generally, the men, at least in the early stages, left to join SWAPO or work in the migrant labour system. The women therefore bore the brunt of the systematic harassment and disruption of their lives, which characterized the military and police presence. Wilhelmina describes the difficulties women experienced in maintaining their families and farms:

> The men have left the country. They are killed; they are in the police zone [the area south of the 'war zone']; they don't want to come back again because some of them are afraid, and now the women have to be at home, educate their children alone at home. And most of them have no money to pay for the children for instance at school. That is why you see there are many children who are doing correspondence, because they can't pass the examination. It doesn't mean that they have no gifts for that, but sometimes it is because they have not money.

An elderly woman living near Ombalantu whose face was still swollen from the last time she was beaten up described the intimidation that regularly occurred:

> I have been beaten up four times now. Once because I went to get some water from the well and it was too late as it was after five. Another time they asked me where I saw SWAPO. I said I didn't see them but they said "You are so old and you didn't see SWAPO before?" I said "No", so I was beaten up. Another time it was because I was looking at the soldiers in their eyes. They thought I didn't respect them. When they come and search and look for things in the house, you have to follow them because they might take things. They search the house every month or so.

The nightly curfew and restrictive laws made resistance more difficult and life even more stressful, as Wilhelmina again explains:

> The women used to work – they had to stand up for instance at 5 o'clock to go to work in the field or preparing food for their families. Now they can't do it. If you have a sick person at home, you can't bring her or him to the hospital at night. Many people died. Children died because of that. And that is really a problem for the women and those who are pregnant.

To describe adequately the dramatic changes in lifestyle the curfew brought about is difficult. Social life, courtship, and marriages, all part of social patterns, became impossible.

> People are being shot at from SADF airplanes and helicopters if they are seen walking in their villages after 5 o'clock in the afternoon. The occupation troops are under orders to shoot anything that moves during the dusk to dawn curfew. Women cannot cook outside their homes without risking their lives. Children cannot play the usual village games in the

evenings. Traditional ceremonies which take place at night are now a thing of the past.[3]

Toos van Helvoort, training rural health workers in the North, explained the longterm implications on the people's mental health:

> Hypertension is frequent. Doctors say it is normal among black people. We think it is stress from the war. Most families have members in Angola. The mothers are so sad and worried. The schools are closed.[4] They are afraid that the children will flee to Angola to join SWAPO and are afraid they won't reach their destination. They are afraid because of the curfew. The mothers say the children are anxious and tense when the casspirs [the huge military vehicles of the South Africans] come round the school.

Toos tells of incidents that would be comic, were they not so ominous:

> At Umulakula, where the church was destroyed, I was there one day. In the middle of the service one of the benches cracked. All the people ran away, they were so tense. Here on Celebration Sunday, there were lots of people. One mother had a bottle of Ontaku [a traditional drink]. It exploded in the sun. There was a big bang and all the people ran away. Every time there is a crowd, people are nervous.

**Strategies for survival**

Active resistance to this kind of violent oppression is extremely difficult, but women trained to equip themselves better for their survival. First aid and midwifery training combated some of the problems due to the curfew. At the women's office in Ongwediva, courses for the women that Wilhelmina organized include help on war trauma:

> We hold leadership courses which include Bible studies, first aid and hygiene. We help women to use natural foods such as the fruit of the tree embe, so that they can feed their children in time of drought . . . They are also asking to learn more about psychology, to teach us in the courses how to help ourselves. They want to know how to help their family with problems, how to help young people.

The women also came to learn reading skills and English:

> They say they want to read the newspapers. Because they have here newspapers and they don't understand. They want to hear – maybe there is something said in connection with their children abroad.

A less obvious form of anti-colonial resistance lay in the women's adoption of social and family roles normally performed by men, including defending the home. The absence of men from the home – in the migrant labour force, in

PLAN or in exile – as a result of the colonial system and the war against it, and women's acceptance of these roles, ensured that Namibian society and culture have not disintegrated. The determination of these women to remain and maintain the social and family structure has been formidable.

Linked to this role of maintaining the family is the women's resistance to contraception, notably to Depo Provera, which has been administered to black Namibian women without their consent or knowledge and even in some circumstances during rape and torture, as in Jacobina's account.

Women, in their traditional role as carers and educators of their children, have also had to explain to their children the inadequacies of the system, the reasons for war, and so on. They have thus performed a vital politicizing role.

**Support networks**

The third form of resistance, without which PLAN's guerrilla activity would have been impossible, was that of actively supporting and sheltering SWAPO combatants, for which the women suffered heavy penalties. Messages and arms, hidden in clothing, were carried from place to place, combatants were sheltered and fed, arms and ammunition stored, all helping to maintain vital links of communication. This support in the field is always essential to guerrilla strategy, and it is women at home who must decide to shelter or give food to the guerrillas and who risk being tortured and killed as a result.[5]

The heroism of individuals engaged in this type of resistance, which by its nature is clandestine, is seldom recognized. The stories women tell of these activities are only now emerging, as Namibia becomes a safer place in which to speak openly. But the punishment and torture inflicted on suspicion of such activity was widespread and made no discrimination between the active and the non-active. Elisabeth Namundjebo recalls:

> I was chained to the wall, legs and arms apart, and they gave me electric shocks to my fingers and toes. I started haemorrhaging. I was taken to hospital and operated on. In jail I was tied to the wall, my feet and ankles are still not healed – they are swollen. After hospital I was given shocks in a chair, with a cloth in my mouth. I was told I had an internal infection and had to go back to hospital. They were accusing me of being SWAPO.

Rauna Nambinga's ordeal in Oshakati prison was similar:

> Electricity was attached to the little fingers of both my hands. It was switched on and off. . . . A rope was tied round my neck and pulled. I fell down unconscious. When I woke I was in a pool of blood and realized that I had broken my jaw and blood was running. I asked for a doctor but was told I was not going to be given one until I told the truth. . . . Then they started with their electrical instruments; this time it was administered on my breasts. It went on for almost three hours.[6]

It must be remembered that these women performed tasks and underwent torture without any of the training and preparation that was offered to combatants.

### Women combatants

Women played a significant role in all aspects of SWAPO organization, including that of active combat. That women refused to be restricted to supportive functions, such as medics and couriers, but were fully trained and equipped as combatants, is clear evidence of a change in the perception of women's role within the movement. This full integration of women was as a result of consistent pressure by the SWAPO Women's Council to be fully and equally involved in the struggle at all levels. Women underwent the same training as men in SWAPO and occupied positions at all levels. Accounts arising from this experience will begin to emerge, as will its consequences for women's perception of themselves and of their roles in independent Namibia.

### Political resistance

Women have been at the forefront of resistance since the beginning of German occupation (see chapter 6 for more details), participating in, and leading demonstrations, rallies and strikes and so on. In August 1988 Hilda Shifidi and Victoria Mweuhanga who, as a result of beatings by white South African troops, had lost their father and husband respectively, took the case to court; but despite the Attorney General laying murder charges the legal process was blocked by P W Botha. Both women have, however, again appealed to the courts.[7]

The importance of women's activities and the threat they were perceived to pose, is indicated by the state's action, in 1973–74, when 2,000 women and young people were forcibly moved from around Windhoek to the North; they were allegedly supporters of SWAPO.[8]

## Effects of war outside the war zone

South of the 'war zone', the situation was somewhat different from that in the North. Conscription at 16 years had been compulsory for black Namibian men since 1981, but this was not enforced in the northern war zones. The colonial government's intention had been to polarize Namibians of different allegiances on a geographical basis as far as possible. Consequently, conscription policy ensured that the majority of conscripts in the 'Namibianized units' of the South-West Africa Territorial Force (SWATF) and Koevoet were from the South of the country.

A strong military presence, although concentrated in the North, was evident throughout the country, along with a corresponding fear of the army and police. Meetings and rallies were regularly repressed forcibly and the courts had extensive powers conferred through the 'security forces'. For example, the Terrorism Act of 1967, provided for indefinite detention for interrogation and allowed for the death sentence to be imposed; and the Protection of

Fundamental Rights Act 1988, provided for prison sentences of up to ten years for boycotting educational establishments or industries, or for 'abstaining from making use of . . . any public service'. This 1988 Act was introduced in response to the student boycott of 1988; neither Act is any longer operational.

In Windhoek in particular, rallies and meetings regularly met with violent suppression. Tear-gas and rubber bullets were commonplace and were used on the student demonstrations in August 1988. Bomb blasts similar to that in Oshakati in February 1988 have occurred in Windhoek and have been blamed on SWAPO. Further South, meetings and rallies are met with similar treatment. During the schools boycott of June 1988 it was reported that:

> Violence broke out at the J.A.Nel secondary school in Keetmanshoop last Sunday when police and army units fired tear-gas into the school grounds to quell a demonstration by striking students who were protesting against police presence on their campus.[9]

In the South the DTA,[10] the pro-government party opposed to SWAPO in the 1989 elections, was heavily promoted. The war in the North was perceived as far away, but the reality of the absence of conscripted sons, or the presence of migrant labourers from the North inevitably brought closer the war and awareness of military occupation.

In the meetings organized by Namibian Women's Voice in Keetmanshoop, the women were not primarily concerned with overt terrorization and war, even though they were often afraid to attend the meetings because of the police. They voiced concerns about apartheid, about family and social disintegration, about alcoholism, women's subordination, and similar issues. Two of the major issues in the North – prostitution and alcoholism – were attributed directly to the war. In addition, it is clear that black women's low social and economic position and the extreme poverty and social disintegration among black Namibians is due both to the war and to the colonial capitalist state in which apartheid as an institution of oppression was state policy.

The connection between the war and the problem of alcoholism among the women is expressed by Dr Tueumuna at Oshakati hospital:

> The main problems for women are the separation of families through exile, detention, war, and so on. This contributes to alcoholism. Drinking in public by women was taboo seven or eight years ago. Now it's common. It has also increased for men.

In the South, as Father Simon at Keetmanshoop Catholic Mission explained, over-indulgence in alchohol also results from frustration:

> If people can't work then they cannot be productive and when you're not productive you become frustrated and your life, your existence becomes meaningless. Because of that, people take to the refuge of the abuse of alcohol which is really a very big and agonizing problem here, and then

because of that, we also have a lot of killings, stabbings, people just killing each other for any nonsensical reason.

The issue of high unemployment in the South will be considered in chapter 2, but it is appropriate to make one comment here. Whether or not high unemployment was deliberate government policy, its value both to the state and economy was to make available a cheap and mobile workforce, and to provide candidates for service in the forces. Prostitution also increased, particularly around the military bases. Sexually transmitted diseases became a growing problem, as did the number of unwanted babies.

These social and domestic problems, common all over the country, are the less overt consequences of war and are particularly disturbing. In the South, where direct effects of the war were more removed, it was perhaps difficult for connections with the war to be recognized and for people to identify the causes for their distress. This can lead to great demoralization among the people.

## Background to the war

From the first German presence in Namibia in the mid-nineteenth century, the occupation has been increasingly militarized. By 1966, when SWAPO launched its armed struggle, there were permanent military bases in the North and South, and five military airports.[11] In 1971, in response to increased activity by SWAPO's military wing, PLAN, thousands of South African military personnel were fighting in Namibia. Little was recorded to acknowledge the extent of PLAN's challenge to the South Africans, but the numbers of garrisons, restricted zones, and soldiers (estimated by 1984 at 100,000 troops and 10,000 militarized police), and the level of military activity clearly indicated that PLAN was a substantial force for the South Africans to counter.[12]

In 1975, military activity was heightened by South Africa's invasion of Angola. In the face of MPLA, the Angolan forces,[13] South Africa retreated and massed its troops, together with those of UNITA,[14] the pro-South African Angolan rebel force, along the thousands of miles of border with Angola. MPLA was supportive of SWAPO and this enabled the guerrilla warfare to continue on a large scale. In addition Namibia then formed a base for South Africa's repeated attacks on MPLA in Angola. The whole of the Northern zone of Namibia – Ovambo, Kavango, Kaokoveld and Caprivi – became a heavily militarized region, with South Africa providing logistical support to UNITA to destabilize and attack the Angolan regime, while simultaneously the South Africans were defending themselves against PLAN. The war with Angola intensified until August 1988 when the South African forces were finally defeated at Cuito Canavale, and had to withdraw to Namibia.

As in all wars, it is the civilians who have perhaps suffered the most. In this war in particular, intimidation of the civilian population was the military forces' clear strategy.

## The South African Forces

Namibia was said to be one of the world's most militarized countries.[15] The South African armed presence in Namibia comprised SADF (South African Defence Force); SAPOL (South African Police); SWATF (South West Africa Territorial Force); and SWAPOL (South West Africa Police) of which an offshoot is 'Koevoet' (the notorious Counter-Insurgency Unit).

SADF comprises largely white South African conscripts who were stationed in Namibia; the South African police personnel also serve with the military. Bases were dotted all over the country, concentrated particularly in the North near the Angolan border, and in the Walvis Bay area that serves as a naval and air base and a training ground.

The front line of fighting is usually taken by SWATF, which was formed in 1974 when a policy of 'Namibianizing' the war was employed. Since 1981, as previously noted, black Namibians were conscripted compulsorily in the South, and voluntarily in the North, with temptingly high salaries by Namibian standards. Although technically SWATF was controlled from Windhoek, it was in effect under the direct control of Pretoria. The strategic aim was to create a pro-South African military force, which would be in a position to destabilize Namibia in the event of independence, with a potential to transform the war for liberation into a civil war.

'Koevoet' is the name for one of SWAPOL's 'special units'. Formed in 1978, its existence was discovered in 1980 by the revelation of a list of assassination targets for the unit. Said to consist mainly of men from the Owambo region, it is a specially trained, highly mobile counter-insurgency unit, known to have perpetrated mass killings; it was the most feared and hated of all the South African forces. Koevoet soldiers disguised as SWAPO fighters, have been responsible for many incidents of murder and torture, and are said to be responsible for 60% of the recorded killings in Owambo. The destruction of St Mary's mission in Odibo is one of the major incidents for which it is widely believed Koevoet were responsible. A pastor who worked at the mission said: 'We followed the casspir tracks back. SWAPO do not have such vehicles.'

Sometimes, members of security forces are called to account for their crimes in the courts. In September 1983:

> Two members of the police special unit "Koevoet" gave evidence in the Windhoek supreme court about one night of bloodshed. Dressed as SWAPO guerrillas, they had moved from kraal to kraal in seach of women and money. Four women had been assaulted and a headman shot.[16]

*The Namibian* reported a case, at Ondangwa magistrates' court, involving Roelof George Freeman, a member of SADF who was fined R800 for:

> Using a firearm in an "irresponsible manner". His appearance was a sequel to an incident on January 1st this year [1987] when Freeman shot and seriously injured a fourteen-year-old girl, Christophina Thomas, for refusing to have sexual intercourse with him.[17]

In early 1989, there was a dispute as to the numbers in Koevoet, as there were urgent calls for its disbandment in the run-up to the November 1989 elections. In February, the South African police commander in Namibia, Dolf de Gouws, stated that 3,000 members of Koevoet had been integrated into the police force. But, on 15 August 1989, in response to international demands, it was announced by Louis Pienaar, the Administrator General, that 1,200 Koevoet would be confined to base; there was no reconciliation of these different figures. There were many calls to disband Koevoet, as their tactics of terrorization were seen as inappropriate to the maintenance of law and order. In his announcement, Mr Pienaar spoke of the 'reorientation and training' planned for Koevoet members; the churches also offered to provide this service. It is evident that this task must be undertaken if, in the future, police and army units are to be respected and trusted by the people.

Koevoet were the worst perpetrators of an officially sanctioned terror campaign that continued throughout the election campaign. Consequently, there was strong criticism of the Administrator General's decision to delay their confinement to base for so long after the 1 April 1984 arrival of UNTAG, his lack of clarity on the numbers of personnel concerned, and the interpretation of 'confinement to base', which has essentially meant: 'Bussing them to and from their homes for the day, leaving them free in the evenings', as the Bishop of Manchester, the Rt. Revd. Stanley Booth-Clibborn reported on 3 September 1989. As for the most part, atrocities by Koevoet have been perpetrated at night, this 'confinement' did little to assuage Namibians' fears. In the run-up to the November 1989 elections, the situation changed daily, and possibilities of either the total confinement of Koevoet or their redeployment were seen as equally plausible.

Koevoet is the most well-known of the 'special units', all of which are highly trained professional units, in some cases employing foreign mercenaries. Others are the top secret 'Recces' or Reconnaissance Commandos, based in South Africa, the 32 Battalion, SWA Task Force and others. In their presentation to the 1984 International Conference on Namibia, the Committee for South African War Resistance stated:

> It is evident from press reports that over the past few years, the special force units have taken on greater responsibility for countering SWAPO activities. This represents a shift in emphasis away from the winning of "hearts and minds" strategy that is publicly propagated by SADF. Heavily armed professional and mercenary units like Koevoet, the Task Force and 32 Battalion rely on swift striking power and work on the principle that the local population are the enemy. That they have acquired such a fearsome reputation for torture and atrocities is a reflection of the desperate methods that SADF is turning to as it slowly but inexorably loses the war in Namibia.[18]

At the time of writing (1988) the war was officially over. In addition to Koevoet, however, other 'special' units and battalions such as SWATF's notorious 101 battalion, which should have been disbanded under the terms of Resolution 435, were still at large, heavily armed, and continuing to intimidate SWAPO supporters, particularly in the North. The Churches' Information and Monitoring Service of the CCN reported in July 1989 that members of battalion 101 said they were on 'temporary leave': 'The battalion 101 members said that they were on standby, that they were armed and were waiting for further instructions.'[19]

Similarly, on 24 July, it was reported in *The Namibian* that SADF bases in the Tsumkwe, Opuwo and Kaoko regions were still operational, that SADF troops were involved in the intimidation of local SWAPO supporters, drives to bar SWAPO from certain areas, planting of landmines and so on.[20]

Another disturbing factor likely to influence future order in the country was the close association between DTA members and the security forces; this was demonstrated by the findings of the Commission for the Prevention of Intimidation, which was itself set up by Louis Pienaar. A SWAPO meeting of 250–300 people was attacked at Okatope in June. The report said: 'The attack was launched alternatively by policemen and DTA supporters working in close collaboration.'

The CCN reported another incident at one of the UN-supervised reception centres for Namibian returnees:

> Late afternoon on August 16th, a convoy of five DTA vehicles drove through Engela [UN reception centre], firing gun bursts at local SWAPO supporters and returnees. The coordinator of the centre, Lutheran pastor Hidipo Shanyengange said that twenty-four people were beaten by the DTA supporters, some seriously. 'One young woman was utterly beaten, blood was all over her clothes, cut with a knife in the face and left breast, stoned in both legs.' One returnee, Tangeni Shikomba, was beaten and abducted from the centre by the DTA mob. Blindfolded and bound, Shikomba was taken away, questioned and pushed out of the truck in front of the local police station. UN police and UNHCR officials who witnessed the scene were unable to intervene – their brief seemed limited to monitoring and not to protecting the returnees.[21]

Clearly, the tactics of the 'security forces', although perhaps differing slightly from unit to unit, have been, and in 1988 continued to be, one of intimidation and terrorization of the civilian population in order to inhibit popular support for SWAPO. These brief details of the situation as it stood in September 1989 are provided in order to illustrate the entrenched nature of the war machinery. Initiating a time of peace will not be easy because, since conscription, families have been split, with members on both sides, and the forces that should normally maintain law and order have been trained for murder and war.

## 'Hearts and Minds'

The 'security forces' were also employed in the so-called 'low-intensity war conflict' with the aim of winning the 'hearts and minds' of Namibians. This strategy, known also as 'civic' or 'social action' was based on the assumption that the PLAN guerrillas depended on the local population for material and psychological support. It has been said that the war was 80% socio-economic and psychological, and 20% military. Through such action the South African forces aimed to isolate the PLAN fighters by gaining support for themselves among the population, and also to strengthen the bantustan administration. It would also mean that the population would be more easily controlled and was seen as a way of securing sources of military intelligence. In 1979, General Lloyd, then commander of the SWATF forces declared: 'The local population is a key factor – its loyalty, goodwill and cooperation will determine the outcome of the struggle. It constitutes the battlefield.' He added that if loyalty could not be secured, 'We will have to move them out of the critical areas.'[22]

The theory of the 'hearts and minds' campaign was that if health, education and public works were developed, the people's quality of life would be improved and they would perceive less reason to support the PLAN forces. In fact, the tactic extended to the deployment of military personnel in hospitals and educational institutions; a move that was far from popular. That the same people who inflicted the injuries were also to heal them aroused resentment as did the fact that employment opportunities were lost as a result of army personnel taking up the positions.

'Hearts and minds' action was introduced in Namibia in 1974 after the military's failure in the North. At the same time violent repression was increased in the North as villages were cleared and areas depopulated, which obviously drew a response contrary to that intended by 'hearts and minds'. Military personnel took up posts as teachers, medics, officials, and so on. Military bases, stationed close to schools and hospitals for 'protection' purposes, were not perceived as such, but met with much popular opposition in the form of strikes, school boycotts and demonstrations. Many school students left the country to join SWAPO in Angola. One such is Paul Ipumbu:

> In 1977 while I was doing my standard nine, a camp was erected about 500 metres from the school at a clinic. And since the camp was erected there we started observing and discovering explosive devices in the surroundings of the school. . . . We reported the matter several times to the base and it looked like they knew exactly where the devices were located and so it was our conviction that they were responsible. . . . I felt my life was endangered. . . . We headed North and we were helped along the way by local inhabitants inside Angola.[23]

The 'hearts and minds' campaign took on different emphasis in different areas. It was concentrated in the North: Owambo, Kavango, Kaokoveld and Caprivi, where support for SWAPO was strongest, and promoted quite strongly in the South, where to win support was easier. In Caprivi, one initiative was the Omega base, set up as a recruiting centre for San people whose traditional means of livelihood had been destroyed by the decimation of the land and restrictions on movement. Tempted by relatively high salaries, and medical facilities they were recruited as soldiers and 'trackers'.

In Kavango, the campaign took the form of improving the infrastructure of military roads and services. This was principally to service the Rundu and Bagani bases from where UNITA was supplied, but was promoted as propaganda in the name of 'developing' the area. In Owambo, where schools and health facilities were controlled by the military,[24] troops had to be withdrawn in 1985 due to the degree of opposition from the bantustan administration. Oswald Shivute, former private secretary to Kalangula, head of the Owambo administration recalls that:

> In '85 Etango [a military 'cultural' organization] was set up and we saw we couldn't cooperate with them. We also chased the army doctors away from the hospitals and the teachers away from the schools.

The 'Etango' that Shivute refers to is one of the 'cultural' organizations created as part of the 'hearts and minds' campaign. Its equivalent in Kavango and Caprivi is 'Ezuva'. Rosalind Namises of the CCN Contextual Theology Unit explains their role:

> They called the other youth groups Ezuva and Etango . . . and then area by area they could identify and get the young people involved. . . . Now in Windhoek we have this one that we call NACOS and NASOK.[25]

The organizations offered training, religious meetings, and so forth, with the aim of recruiting young people:

> Some youth groups were started and young people were called up to these camps and there were some nice things like the clean bedding sheets, food that was very nice and behind that there was this whole hidden agenda, where the young people would meet for a weekend and the training they received was quite military, self-defence type of training. They were shown videos [that] condemned Alan Boesak, Tutu, Kameeta. You remember there was this whole question of necklacing. Those were the things that were shown to the young people. And actually it was to create an atmosphere where young people mostly the boys would join the army. And that was called the "Cadet", and "Veld and Vlei".

In the West was a similar, but smaller organization – Flamingo. In the South, where DTA was strongest, the strategy seems to have been more in the nature of offering goods and setting up small development projects, following on the example of independent women's groups. Often, as Rosalind explains, it is the women, as those responsible for the family, who are affected:

> As mothers they would be again the target of the sewing groups, the new projects that are created. So they got these things unaware, most of them,

because they needed skills. . . . Especially of course we are a very vulnerable community, especially when it comes to food, when it comes to health, when it comes to Christianity. These are the things that we as Namibians need.

As Rosalind mentions, religious sensibilities, by way of right-wing Christianity, were also exploited:

The church that was starting to emerge, the new church, where people were called for repentance, where visitors like Jimmy Swaggart would come to be screened on TV and where all the salvation tents would come inside the country. One of the pastors in the North was a white man who was an ex-soldier. The whole background [was that] of right-wing religion and its control, of course the government would have something to do with it.

But the 'hearts and minds' campaign experienced great difficulty in successfully involving the people. One military commander in Owambo reportedly remarked in 1981: 'In Owamboland I'm not sure the hearts and minds strategy does much good because of the large numbers of SWAPO there.'[26]

According to Rosalind, the strategy failed partly due to an over-estimation of the Namibians' naivety. People automatically mistrusted white administration's initiatives because of its continuing violent, repressive tactics:

The system has been such [that] people just didn't like things that come from the South African government. People just reject even though they don't know its name. . . . What happens is there's a picture of killing, and then a picture of the Good Samaritan. . . . So people would not trust . . . [they] would go and take those things, and then come back home and just stay. . . . The only people involved were the Koevoet, the soldiers that were already involved.

The progressive churches were also instrumental in raising awareness of the implications of such programmes.

Just as the DTA were closely involved with the military, they were closely involved with the hearts and minds campaign (according to Rosalind) as many of them were soldiers or ex-soldiers. They engaged, it seems, both in positive persuasion – food and money – and in intimidation. Rosalind told of one incident in which DTA 'vigilantes' attacked and killed people.

## The Namibian forces – PLAN

South Africa's theoretical policy of winning the 'loyalty' of the local population was a direct attempt to counter SWAPO's policy of guerrilla warfare, through its armed wing, which depended on a strong network of local people.

PLAN was formed in 1966, the first clash was on 26 August in the same year

**Spinner in the carpet factory at Dordabis**

at Omgulumbashe in Owambo. PLAN rapidly increased its activity in the 1970s as a result of the 1971–72 general strike, and the end of Portuguese control of Angola, when Angola was opened up to PLAN, giving them access to the Northern border. A steady stream of Namibians crossed the border, going North to join SWAPO's military wing, particularly at times of increased repression, for example in 1978. In many cases SWAPO directed them to pursue further education rather than to join the ranks of PLAN.

Initially, the combatants emphasized their political role, of integrating, organizing and mobilizing among the local population in Namibia, as is illustrated by an excerpt from SWAPO's political programme: 'We do not beautify war as a purpose or regard it as a form of sport. We see war for what it is – an extension of politics by other means'.[27]

When Angola became available as a base, PLAN's military activities increased, using guerrilla sabotage techniques and keeping thousands of South African troops occupied in Northern Namibia. In the rainy season, when cover is better, combatants penetrated further South, attacking white farms, police bases, communication networks, and similar targets. The popular support necessary for this was even recognized by the South African officials (although information as to the level of fighting was always heavily suppressed) who, in 1974, acknowledged that SWAPO:

> Has an intelligence gathering network whereby the public, especially the hundreds of cuca [trading] shops in Owambo and Kavango are involved and keep it informed as to the movement of the security forces.[28]

Women and men have equal status in PLAN, as part of SWAPO's policy of equality for women. Putuse Appollus described how many of the young women arrived at the SWAPO camps and wanted to go straight to fight:

> Many of the girls say we can have an education later, we want to go and fight with the others. But we only let women between the ages of nineteen and thirty go. On the front all the work is shared without question. Everyone takes their turn in the hunting, skinning and cooking of the animals. They all wear the same uniform . . . It's a matter of "comrade", a communal sort of life without the sexist division. In fact the women are so good at shooting, they often beat the men.[29]

It was largely through the sustained efforts of PLAN's guerrilla war in Namibia, coupled with the combined forces of Angolan, Cuban and SWAPO troops fighting the South Africans and UNITA in Angola, that the war became so expensive for South Africa, and eventually led to their defeat at Cuito Cuanavale in August 1988.

Namibian women have had to work hard against forces of social disintegration prevalent throughout the country. It was part of their relentless resistance to domination, seen most overtly in the war and the state's policy of directing military force against the civilian population.

# 2. 'You only work to survive'

## The economy

If the war was the most obvious manifestation of South Africa's colonialism, the economic violence inflicted by Namibia's occupiers has perhaps been even more damaging; it will certainly be more serious and far-reaching in its effects. Describing the role of women in Namibia's economy at the time of writing (1988) and how they have been forced into situations of extreme poverty, hardship and sometimes degradation risks presenting them as passive victims of the system, but as later chapters will show this is not the case. An understanding of the economic conditions under which women live (often barely managing to survive) is essential in order to understand their struggles.

The introduction describes how the Namibian economy has been structured in a way beneficial both to its white rulers and (in so far as they are distinct) to its colonial master and its allies. Black Namibians have been forced, directly or indirectly, to participate in this system. For most women this has meant very restricted alternatives: employment at starvation wages, unemployment in the townships, or subsistence farming in the reserves. Employers took advantage of the low wages paid to black women by using their labour rather than men's. Black women's labour has provided leisure time for white women, and unemployment has helped keep labour costs low. Black women's enforced abandonment on the reserves has also contributed to low wage levels and the triumph of the whole bantustan system. All black Namibian women have in some way been affected by an economy constructed for whites.

The burden of survival in these conditions has been heavier for women than for men. That women's wages are far lower than men's leads to an added hardship, as frequently a man cannot find work, or he abdicates responsibility for his children, thus leaving their mother to support them. Even women in a reasonable financial position have to take on the household's domestic work and care of the children, whether or not they are in paid work.

### Women in paid employment

Usually through necessity rather than choice, Namibians have taken up paid employment in the colonial economy. From the early days of South African rule, residents of the North were taxed in order to force them to earn money by taking contract work. Any attempt to 'break contract' was severely dealt with. The system was underpinned by growing land hunger in the reserves so that the population as a whole eventually became dependent on the wages of migrants.

Contract workers from the North were almost exclusively men, leaving the women behind to work the land, but in the South women were much more involved in the commercial economy. In 1948 the South West African Native Labour Commission, set up by the authorities, found that many women in this area were in part-time work and that the men were fully employed.[1]

These patterns of employment in Namibia remained largely unchanged until independence, although there have been some adjustments; perhaps the biggest shift was the high level of unemployment in the South in 1988–89. This was not the case earlier, when the labour shortage experienced by farmers and mine-owners led directly to the establishment of the migrant labour system. Unchanged, however, is the fact that although many women are in paid employment, the female waged workforce is much smaller than the male. Government statistics are unreliable, but one writer estimates that 85,000–100,000 women are in waged work.[2] Another puts the figure at 73,000 against a male workforce of 172,000.[3] The majority of these women would probably agree with Martha, a resident of Katutura supporting seven children: 'You only work to survive. What I earn is only just enough to keep my children alive'.

The range of jobs open to women is strictly limited, with the greatest demand for their labour in the domestic and agricultural sectors. A majority of white families in Namibia employ a black 'maid', 'servant' or 'girl' who works long hours for low pay. Women make up a large part of the workforce on white-owned farms in the South, sometimes as part of a family unit, and are often employed as part-time or seasonal workers.[4]

In factories, employers are changing their workforce from men to women in order to cut costs by paying lower wages. The workforce at the Table Top fish factory in Walvis Bay, for instance, is female; that the factory opened only in 1982 is significant.[5] Meat processing factories in Windhoek are also staffed by women. Conversely, Vinnia Ndadi's account of factory work in the town in the 1950s implies a male labour force based on the contract system.[6]

Women are also employed in shop and office work. Black women have only recently begun to enter these areas, which were previously occupied by white and 'coloured' women. Professional careers are almost entirely limited to teaching and nursing which, while they carry a relatively high status, do not generally allow women opportunities for advancement. There are very few black women school principals, for instance, and until people returned from exile in 1988, there was only one black woman doctor in the country.[7]

Not all women who work for money fall within the scope of the formal economy. Some engage in trading or production of commodities such as *tombo* (beer), cakes and baskets either to earn an income or raise their wages to subsistence level; others are forced into prostitution. These activities have usually been illegal under the colonial regime, and have therefore involved a high degree of risk. There is also a great deal of child labour in this area; its extent is unknown, but court records class black children as young as seven as 'unemployed'.[8]

The day-to-day duties carried out by women in each sector differ widely, but generally the conditions of their employment have a number of common features. Mainly, these are: hours and conditions; vulnerability in employment; racism, and sexual harassment; low wage levels.

**Hours and conditions**

'Domestic workers are still their bosses' property', said Erika Ramakhutla, a SWAPO Women's Council speaker, at a 1988 May Day rally. 'They are no better than his dog'.

Workers in Namibia under South African rule had very little legal protection from the exploitation that was rife in all sectors. The 1982 Conditions of Employment Act in effect confirmed existing practices with respect to working hours and other conditions, rather than attempting to halt abuses; neither did the Act attempt to counteract earlier repressive legislation. The affiliation of trade unions to a political party was also banned; and the 1982 Act failed to deal with such issues as a minimum wage and maternity leave. Moreover, it did not apply to the most vulnerable of all Namibian workers, those in the domestic and agricultural sectors.[9] In 1988, employment legislation was under review by a Commission headed by the South African Professor Wiehahn. The Commission had not reported, however, by the beginning of the implementation of 435 (see chapter three).

The majority of women in paid employment – concentrated in domestic and agricultural work – have thus had no legal protection. This factor, and the high levels of unemployment making finding another job difficult, have tended to make women virtual slaves to their employers. Representatives of the domestic workers' committee in Tsumeb described their work-load: 'We have hard times with our employers. We just have to work hard for low wages, and we don't even have holidays. . . . We have to work from 8am to 6pm, five days a week, and sometimes we must work Saturdays and Sundays as well'.

Eva, a domestic worker employed by Tsumeb Corporation Ltd to work for one of its white staff, said: 'I work an eight-hour day, six days a week. You have to work all eight hours without a break or teatime, and you are not even allowed to go to the café to buy yourself some food'.

A further hardship for many domestic workers is that they must live in the employer's house, caring for her children, while not permitted their own family life. 'I am not allowed to have my own children with me in Windhoek', said one, 'while I look after my employer's child. I miss my children all the time. . . . ' But if she went home (to the rural area) to see them, she had 'even less money to send home for food'.[10]

Women who live in townships have other problems.

> We must leave our children during the day because there are no centres to look after them. . . . We work for the white housewife – we have to look after

> her children, while we leave our children at home. . . . When we come home, we don't know whether they have been to school. . . . And we don't know whether they have eaten. Most of the time children go to the dustbins to scratch for food.[11]

These conditions are leading to a growing number of street children (see chapter 4).

Added to the stress created by these conditions is the sheer volume of work expected of women. Victoria, of the domestic workers' committee in Tsumeb, said, 'When we come home, we have to look after our children and clean the house'. Her colleague Frieda had the same problem: 'I have three children, and every day I have to wash their nappies, and the work is too much'. Lack of transport is a further problem for domestic workers living out: 'We have no means of transport to or from work', said Eva, 'we just walk. And then if you arrive late at work, even just a few minutes, you get a complaint form, and if you do it a second time, that is the end'.

Most women living in the townships have similar childcare and transport problems, and those employed in other sectors also experience long hours of work without a break. Employers in the meat processing industry, for instance, work in sub-zero temperatures, sometimes for a 16-hour day.[12] Martha, who worked in a meat factory in Windhoek, described how:

> It was really tough work. We had to start at twelve midnight and knock off at eight in the morning. We worked very hard and long hours, irrespective of our other duties at home, caring for our children and so on. If you missed a day's work, or if you came late, they simply subtracted it from your salary without listening to your reasons . . .

Conditions of work for most Namibian women mean long hours, hard labour and little job satisfaction or financial reward, as a domestic worker summed it up:

> I do all the housework, gardening, washing, ironing and cooking. I get no free time, and nothing which makes me happy. There is a terrible lot of work, but very little pay. I also work on Saturdays and Sundays.[13]

Perhaps employees on white-owned farms experience the harshest conditions. These workers usually live in corrugated iron shacks and are considered as virtually the farmer's property and expected to labour from dawn till dusk. A priest at Keetmanshoop stated that normally these workers' only day off was Christmas Day, and that they were 'the poorest of the poor'.

Women are employed on these farms both as domestic workers and as workers on the land. They are part of the resident community of labourers, living in family units, and apparently also engage in seasonal work. Because of the extreme isolation of these workers, there are few ways in which they can communicate their problems and information is scarce.

**Vulnerability**

> At TCL, if a lady gets pregnant, she is automatically fired without any pension or any pay. Some of the ladies started to work for TCL at a young age, and up to now they are without children because they are afraid of being fired.

Maternity leave has been the exception rather than the rule, and women in all occupations have suffered. Reports of dismissal due to pregnancy are common, and apply to women in most sectors. Even teachers and nurses have had to resign if they became pregnant. An extreme case is outlined in reports that, at one company in Oshakati (owned by the First National Development Corporation, partly owned by the state) women had to work until they actually went into labour, at which point they were fired; not all were reinstated.[14]

This attitude on the part of employers further demonstrates how the system has viewed black women as objects, useful only for their labour, and recognizing no responsibility for their welfare or that of their families; the term 'girl' used to describe domestic workers is an indication of this attitude.

Employment legislation has allowed a worker to be dismissed for any reason at all if a month's notice is given. But, as we have already noted, the meagre protection offered by this legislation is available to very few women. Dismissal without any kind of compensation can result from, for example, breakages, lateness, asking for a pay increase or for a contract, and refusing to have sex with an employer. Maria, a resident of Tsumeb, was not sacked for any of these reasons, but apparently because her employer suddenly became aggressive. Eventually the two women quarrelled and Maria was instantly dismissed. 'I cleaned the house, I did everything in the house, she left the house for me', said Maria. She had held the job for 22 years.

**Racism and sexual harassment**

Racial abuse of workers has been commonplace. 'Such words as "kaffir" are used against us in our jobs', reported Eva. 'You have no right to touch the boss's property. . . . You are not even allowed to use the boss's toilet. And what they often say is, that the kaffir is just a kaffir'.

Professional women's working conditions are slightly better than those in lower status jobs, but they have been equally victims of racism. Agnes Tjongarero, a nurse at Katutura State Hospital, said, 'Even the way the white doctors, the matrons and sisters used to talk to the black patients and to us was as if we were just things'.

Racism has not been restricted to verbal abuse; it has been implicit in the whole structure of white domination. While not all workers were abusively treated all were trapped in a racist system. As Frieda, of the domestic workers' committee in Tsumeb said, employers 'know they pay us too low wages, so they are friendly with us and treat us well'.

Employers' patronizing treatment of their workers is another manifestation of racism. It has been common practice for domestics and agricultural workers to be given clothes and food in lieu of a fair wage. 'She took old milk which had been in the fridge for a long time, and some vegetables', said Maria, 'and asked me if I wanted them or not. I told her that I do not eat things like that at my place'. Live-in domestic workers were subject to similar treatment. According to a migrant worker, if their 'room has a mat in it they take it out because they say you are going to waste it, and that you are not a fit person to sleep on it'.[15]

Sexual and racial discrimination against job applicants has also been widespread. According to Amelia, a black woman living in Oranjemund, 'full apartheid exists'.

> There are salary differences between blacks and whites, and there is discrimination against women [seeking employment] in teaching and nursing. My colleague and I both came here in 1978–79, and we were promised jobs which didn't materialise. In the shop, black workers must have standard 8 and know English and Afrikaans. This is not required of whites.

Sexual harassment, by its clandestine nature, tends to remain unrecognized. 'The missus smokes one cigarette after another', said one domestic worker, 'and I follow her all over the house . . . to remove the ashes. And the boss fondles my breasts. . . . '[16] Often women are forced into sex with an employer in order to gain or keep a job.

While it is not to be expected that this form of oppression will automatically disappear with the coming of independence, it is clearly a manifestation of white domination and black women's powerlessness to resist an employer's demands when the need to keep a job could make the difference between life and death for herself and her children. It is to be hoped that independence will make whites more accountable for their actions and establish more safeguards for women, making it easier for them to resist such enforced prostitution.

**Low wage levels**

In Namibia wages have been low for all black people, and still lower for women than for men. Frieda said: 'I work in two jobs, and I'm paid R60 per month for each – R120 altogether. Anna is paid R80, and Victoria R100'. The average rent for these women was R25 per month. With bills for water and electricity, school fees, clothing and food to provide, they could barely make ends meet. Subsistence levels and the poverty resulting from low pay will be considered later.

Pay levels are extremely variable according to area, employer and job. The wage levels quoted above are, in fact, higher than the average quoted for domestic workers in most published sources, which give R20 as the minimum.[17] Agricultural work may be assumed as similarly or even more badly paid. Other jobs for women have been slightly more remunerative. Pay rates for black shop workers are given as between R50 and R120; R200–250 for office staff (although whites were paid substantially more for the same work); and R300–500 for nurses and teachers.[18] Nursing and teaching represent women's highest earning power, but they do not compare particularly well to the wages available to men in the commercial economy. For example, one man, on the lowest pay grade at the diamond mine in Oranjemund, said he had taken that job instead of continuing his career as a teacher because he was able to earn more.

These figures may be seen in perspective by noting the wage levels recorded in a 1986 survey of Katutura conducted by the Catholic church (and therefore more reliable than government statistics). Researchers found that average pay in Katutura ranged between R100 and R300 per month, while 69% of the waged population earned less than R300.[19] These figures applied to both men and women and the latter's average earnings can be expected to be much less. It should, however, be noted that the earnings of a small minority of women are well above these levels, or that some are supported by very well-paid men. The 1980s have seen the authorities' deliberate creation of a black middle class in an attempt to minimize the grievances of a section of the population. But this development has been of no value to the majority of women.

If a common complaint against the migrant labour system has been that it enabled employers to avoid paying a living wage for a worker and his dependants, the same charge can be levelled in respect to women's employment. Women are either excluded from areas of male waged labour (for instance, in the mines) or paid less for the same work. That employers have begun to see the advantages of this differential is demonstrated by the employment of female rather than male labour in some parts of the fish and meat processing industry. In 1988 a similar move was in progress in the diamond-mining town of Oranjemund, where previously the domestic labour force had been exclusively male, employed directly by CDM, the mining company, and paid around R400 per month. The company was proposing to substitute these workers with women employed by a second company, LTA, contracted to CDM. Teresa, a (black) medical worker in the town, explained that 'the fee to LTA for each worker will be only R230 per month'. The implication was that the amount actually paid to each woman for her labour would be much less.

## Unemployment

There are no reliable figures of those unable to find paid work. The concept of unemployment is in itself fluid, if to the jobless in the townships are added those working the land in the bantustans because they are unable to find other employment. One estimate reckoned that 20% of the black workforce was wholly unemployed, while many more were underemployed or able only to obtain seasonal work.[20] In 1986, unemployment in Katutura was said to be running at 43%.[21] The problem is perhaps even more severe in the South. In Keetmanshoop, for example, there is little besides domestic work for the women and men's employment is said to be confined to a single brick factory.

Unemployed women have often been forced into trading or prostitution. In the towns trading has usually been illegal and women have constantly risked being picked up by the police. Prostitution was sometimes the only method of surviving for young girls as well as women. 'The going price for a child prostitute', said a social worker in Katutura, 'is R10, while adult prostitutes charge between R20 and R50. So you see, the men, whites and black alike, often take the young girls because they are cheaper'.[22] For others, the only option left is begging.

## Bantustans, migrant labour and women

In the introduction, we refer to the migrant labour system and the underlying reasons for its enforcement. The family break-up, starvation and illness caused by this system have been some of the ugliest ways the white minority have informed the black majority that they were expendable.

Life in the reserves is hard. There is a shortage of land, and these areas are used as a dumping-ground for the sick, the elderly and the children whom the white economy has no interest in supporting. A 1983 estimate found that fewer than a quarter of those living in the reserves were engaged in productive work. Moreover, as most contract work has been available only to men, as we have noted, the women have been left to survive from their farms and whatever their men could afford to send them. In 1980–81 there were about 70,000 more women than men in the 'homelands'.[23]

The creation of the bantustan system in itself meant great hardships both for Namibian women and men. To achieve the present situation, in which 77% of the farmland is owned by whites,[24] there were widespread forced removals of the people. Miss Gowases, an old-age pensioner now living in the black township of Tsumeb, described how her family was forced to move off their lands while she was still a child.

> My parents lived on a farm near here, and they had a herd of cattle and goats and so on. Then the government told them that they must go to another reserve. The government's argument was that they had too many livestock. But later the people died out, and also the stock, and only I survived. Now I have nothing.

As a woman farmer said, 'When we lost our land, we lost our rights, our family way of life, our independence and our culture'.[25]

For women, one specific consequence of the migrant labour system was that the money men earned they also controlled and they usually gave priority to their own needs and leisure. Men thus had access to the cash economy denied to women, thus increasing the power gap between sexes.[26] A number of factors, including the poor quality of the land and overcrowding, have led to the increased dependence of families in the reserves on migrants' earnings; this, as we have seen, was deliberate policy on the part of the South African authorities. It has been estimated, for example, that in 1976 over 50,000 people relied for support on the earnings of 9,400 black migrant workers in Walvis Bay.[27]

Men themselves have recognized the destructive effects of the contract system, and calls for its end have been a constant theme of the union movement. Workers in Tsumeb stated that migrant labour, 'touches us because a man has to come and work in the South, while his family is far away. Maybe he has the chance to be with his family just a week per year – just a few days'. Similarly, a worker taking part in a 1972 survey protested that 'we do not know why a person has to be separated from his wife for twelve months. It means much, much longing. And later the man commits adultery. . . . Because of the contract my children do not know me. When I return home the children flee from me'.[28] An end to the system was one of the demands of the general strike of 1971–72.

The women have not only suffered similar emotional and physical deprivation, they have also had to cope with running the homestead, doing back-breaking farm work, taking sole responsibility for the children including caring for them in sickness and, during the war, continual danger of violence and harassment. Wilhelmina Shikomba, the Lutheran women's officer at Ongwediva, who grew up on a farm described how, 'I had to hoe at the time for hoeing, pound corn, and help my mother cook. We had to walk for half an hour to fetch water, and half an hour back again.' If this was the work expected from a girl, her mother's burden was clearly much heavier.

Women in the bantustans whose men are unable, or refuse, to send them money, or are dead, have the most arduous existence. A group of village women in the Kavango explained that:

> Single mothers have experienced a lot of problems here. They are alone in their house with their children. They don't have a husband to help them . . . they have to do all the work on their own: work in the field, maybe catch fish and do all kinds of work in the house when the children are at school. And sometimes there is hunger at home and they have to go and do some work for somebody so that they can get some mealie-meal for the family to survive.[29]

The life of single mothers who for one reason or another have been deprived of land, is even more desperate. Johanna, living in central Namibia with ten children, who has to live by begging from her almost equally poor neighbours, explained:

> Long ago, my husband went to Windhoek to look for work, but he is unemployed so he never sends money. I get a relief ration from the government each month . . . but it only lasts four days, so I live by begging for the rest of the month. I send the children out to beg for small amounts of food.[30]

The family was living at near-starvation level.

That women in the bantustans, whose lives are typified by constant drudgery and struggle, have survived, brought up their children and contributed to the wider struggle for independence is a testimony to their courage and resourcefulness. While the migrant system has been infinitely harmful, it may, paradoxically, have stimulated, or forced, some women to achieve a measure of self-reliance that otherwise, had their husbands been at home, they would not have achieved. How far these social changes will affect women's lives and status in the long term, after independence, remains to be seen.

Some women have survived not by staying in the reserves, but, sometimes with their children, have gone to live illegally with their men in the townships, where there was a possibility of obtaining work and they did not have to live a separated life. Accommodation is a severe problem, and many women have had to move into the 'single quarters' that house the migrant workers in Namibia's townships. In Swakopmund, for example, many families live in the man's small room, the man and woman sharing the single bed while the children sleep on the floor; such families always risk police raids.

## The results of exploitation

In 1986 the minimum subsistence level for each household in Katutura was R394 per month, excluding rent; a minimum monthly salary of R604 was recommended for the head of a household of six people. As we have seen, the average actual wage of Katutura residents, at R100–R300, fell far short of this sum.[31] Earlier studies reveal a similar gap between needs and earning power. In 1983 the minimum subsistence level was estimated at R301.48 per month, while the actual average family income was said to be only R98. According to another survey in the same year, 86% of black workers in Windhoek were living below subsistence level, and the figure for the North was 99%.[32]

The Namibian people live in desperate poverty, with insufficient food or housing, and frequently, inadequate sanitation and water services. Access to health care and education is severely restricted. Deprivation has, in many cases, led to social problems such as alcoholism, delinquency and family break-up, while the lack of educational opportunities locks the children of the poor into poverty. Erika, of the SWAPO Women's Council, explained that

> women experience many problems: inadequate housing, lack of childcare facilities, inadequate schooling for the kids, and lack of transport facilities. Taxation . . . is not used for improving our standard of living, but is used against us . . . to fund the army and police.

Similarly, representatives of Namibia Women's Voice in Keetmanshoop, where conditions are even worse than in Katutura, described how, 'Children don't attend school. The parents don't know, because they are out early and work late. The kids don't get proper food or sleep, and they need to find jobs or crime to supplement the family's income.'

> Housing is a problem. Wages average R30–40 per month, and often a

> woman has no husband and is supporting six children on a single income. All the money goes on rent, and people are evicted when they can't pay. Many then erect a shanty house in the backyard of a friend. They must also pay for this.

One of the strongest ironies of the Namibian situation is how, throughout the country, black townships have been juxtaposed with white settlements. Comfortably out of sight of the white towns, the black and 'coloured' locations are nevertheless close enough to enable black workers to travel to town every day to work for the whites. In the process, black Namibians have been constantly aware of the contrast between the luxurious living conditions enjoyed by their employers, and the deprivation and overcrowding of the townships. White Namibians enjoy a very high material standard of living, expressed through large houses, expensive cars and the surplus income to employ domestic workers.

The breakdown in social structures caused by this widespread poverty, and related factors such as the migrant labour system, have become of great concern to social workers and other members of the community. Lindy Kazombaue, a social worker of the Catholic church and a representative of Namibia Women's Voice, described the family problems of Katutura:

> Abuse of men [by their employers] at work leads to violence in their own families, drinking and so on. Maybe women also take it out on their children. There is delinquency among children, because of lack of personal attention to them. Single parenting is also prevalent. Most women have five or six kids from different men. Very few get married, and they have financial problems: most women are domestic workers. There are no strict laws about maintenance payments from the fathers. Single parenting is also caused because husbands die, and because of the migrant labour system. The role of the father is very unclear. Most of the nation is brought up by women alone.

The proportion of families headed by women in Katutura is estimated at between 60 and 70%.[33]

Father Simon, of the Keetmanshoop Catholic mission, laid responsibility for social breakdown on unemployment and poverty. He concluded that, 'All these things are caused by the fact that people have nothing to do. They have no work, and they have to find some outlet'. He was convinced that these social ills were due to 'This abject apartheid system, which has caused the largest portion of our people in this country to live a subhuman type of existence'.

As we have seen, alcoholism and other social problems are attributable to the war as well as to economic conditions; in so far as poverty is caused by the war, and represents aggression against the Namibian people, the cause is the same. Chapter four considers its effect on health.

Another factor that has exacerbated the poverty of women compared to men is the operation of traditions concerning inheritance in some ethnic groups, for example the Owambo. Nangula Kathindi, worker at the Women's Desk at the

Council of Churches, explained that tradition dictates that children belong to their mother's clan and have no claims on that of their father. When a man dies, his relatives may take all his possessions, leaving the widow and children with nothing.

> If your husband dies, the relatives who have never visited you, or those who have never had contact with you, will come and inherit things if they were close to him. It's a very tough battle sometimes. We have heard of situations where even clothing was taken from women when their husbands died. Another problem is housing. Usually even the house is taken from the wife when the husband dies, especially land in the North. And then it is so difficult for this woman to get money from anywhere, to get land again to live on with her children.[34]

Township women are also victims of these inheritance customs. Rarely are men affected in this way, because the household's property is usually deemed to belong to the husband. Women often have no property defined as their own, although they may have worked as hard or harder than their husbands for it.

Undoubtedly, some women have turned to alcohol abuse and other forms of self-destruction, but the general effect of social breakdown has been to shift responsibility from men to women. The enforced separation of husbands and wives, the inability of men to deal with the impact of unemployment on their personal lives, and women's traditional role in caring for their families, have meant that women have increasingly taken on the task of providing for their children and often their husbands and parents. That so many women have managed to do so is an achievement that must not be overlooked in the future.

## Social services

Very little assistance has been available to Namibia's poor. Help from the state has been minimal; churches and other organizations, while doing their best to respond to the need, realize that they cannot fill the gap left by inadequate government systems.

Theoretically, a pension is payable to people over the age of 60, but in practice many do not receive it. Mrs Shanghala, a resident of the North, explained that because she did not have the right papers she was deprived of the pension.

> I went to Ondangwa [to the Owambo Administration offices] to try to get my pension. Because the birth date on my ID is wrong I took my membership card from the church. But the people from Ondangwa just took my membership card and put it in the dustbin, and then looked at the ID and said "No, you are not 60. You must go back". I have been there four times now.

For those declared eligible, the procedure for distributing the pensions has often proved an obstacle for those entitled to receive it. In Owambo, for example, they were forced to travel once a month in person to centres where South African soldiers handed out the money. The level of the pension has also been inadequate, in some cases as low as R50 per month, and this may be the only income for a whole family. Miss Gowases, who was supporting four grandchildren explained:

> I get a pension of R65. It is definitely not enough for me, but I have no other alternative, so I must take it. I have the children of a daughter who died recently. The social workers came to my home in 1981 and asked me to take the children. They said they would give me financial help, but up to now they never gave me the promised money. I am continuing to help these children, but because of this very low pension money I can't afford it. The government is very unfair, because in the black community they know that people have a lot of children, but they are giving such a small pension.

One peculiarity of the pension system has been that, because the pension has been paid by the ethnically-based bantustan authorities, the amount has been dependent on the recipient's ethnic group. Central government provided a fixed sum of R50 per pensioner to these authorities, and they added what they could. The authorities for blacks have been less well-funded than those for whites and 'coloureds', as their revenue has come from the poorest section of the population. Consequently pensions paid to their beneficiaries have been much lower. According to Lindy Kazombaue, 'some black people get only R50 per month, while "coloureds" get R150 and whites R270.'

Administration through ethnic authorities has not only perpetuated economic inequalities, but also led to an absence of social services due to technicalities. In the case of the squatter settlement under the Rehoboth government, the spokesman explained that because they received no finances from the central or ethnic authorities,

> It is difficult for us to service these people. Under the Rehoboth Self Government Act anybody who lives here is our responsibility, but those squatters who are Nama/Damara speakers pay taxes to their own ethnic authorities – to the Ovambo or Damara administrations.[35]

There have been some other state handouts, made on a fairly erratic basis and evidently completely inadequate for the level of need. 'There are some state social workers based at the hospital', said Anna, a Katutura resident. 'State handouts appear to be made arbitrarily, except that women whose husbands are dead appear to be favoured.'

Related to the state services have been non-governmental organizations with an unacknowledged connection with the authorities. 'Cultural' organizations, for example, have given out food and other goods, as has the South African-backed political party, the DTA. The Namibian Red Cross, also linked with the

**Market in northern Namibia**

MAYDAY
NAMIBIA
OUR
WAGES

'government', although presenting itself as a bona fide welfare organization, is in fact unrelated to the International Red Cross and is connected only to the South African Red Cross. Following is Martha's experience of it:

> I thought I should approach these people at the Red Cross. I am now mother to seven children, and my husband has been out of work for eight years now. I have to provide alone for the whole family, and I also have a problem with my right leg – I cannot stand for long periods. So I found a white lady there at the Red Cross offices and explained all my problems to her. She told me to come back the next day. The following day the women said, "No, if you feel you can't manage with all those children, send some of them to the army so that they can look after themselves and also look after you". I refused – I would rather face the suffering I am in up till now. I was shocked. I thought the Red Cross was there to assist people like me, but I was just told to send my children to the army.

Other welfare provision for the poor has come from the churches and the International Red Cross, which in particular has provided food and blankets to war victims. During the especially severe drought of 1988, the Council of Churches in Namibia was active in getting relief supplies to the people affected. The churches have also been very important in providing health and education services. Of enormous significance, too, is the extended family system which is still very strong in Namibia. Although the system is criticized on a number of counts, it is doubtless the wage earners' sense of responsibility towards their relatives that has kept many people from starvation. An example of the effectiveness of this system is the way in which the vast majority of the 40,000 exiles who returned to Namibia in 1989 were absorbed back into their families. Often they had been away for more than ten years, and their arrival added to the overcrowding of the townships, but they were welcomed with open arms.

But the extended family cannot guarantee a good living for all when pay levels are low, and none of the schemes for immediate relief of the symptoms of poverty has been as important or as effective as the resistance of Namibians to the exploitation that has caused it.

# 3. 'Let us stand together'

## The unions

Namibia's dynamic and constantly growing workers' movement has resulted from the exploitation to which white rule has subjected all black Namibians. The effectiveness of the unions' power is to be seen not only in concessions made by employers but also their capacity to call workers out on strike. Namibian women respond as warmly as men to the call for workers' organization and perceive unions to be relevant to their situation. One domestic worker said, 'We have no one to look after the children [while at work], and still we are supposed to remain content'.[1]

### Women in the unions

'Women in the union are stronger than men', said Sena Rautenbach, a shop steward in NAFAU, the food workers' union. 'They are more keen to take action'.[2]

The relatively small number of women within the unions makes their militancy particularly impressive. According to Loide Kassingo, an organizer of the National Union of Namibian Workers (NUNW):

> The proportion of women in the unions is very low compared to the men. This is because of the political, social and economic situation, which means that more men are employed than women, and it's also because women have domestic work at home and don't have time to be in the union. But in NAFAU, NAPWU (the public workers' union) and NANTU (the teachers' union) there is a significant percentage of women. NAPWU and NAFAU both have women members of their national executive and central committees.

This view was endorsed by Barnabas Tjizu, leader of the NUNW in 1988:

> Except for domestic workers, women are in the minority in most jobs. This is especially true in the metalwork industry, where women are mainly employed as teamakers, cleaners and errand-runners. In MANWU (the metalworkers' union), female membership is maybe 50 out of 4000.

Despite their low numbers, women do occupy leadership positions, particularly in the unions with a higher female membership. Sena Rautenbach holds high positions within NAFAU and NUNW; Cecilia Paulus is national secretary of NAPWU (second in the hierarchy). According to Tjizu, in 1988 the vice-chairperson of MANWU in Windhoek was a woman, and workers' committees in NAFAU had women leaders. Cecilia explained that women were keen to be involved because:

> They feel that the union is answering their needs. It's where you can find people to solve your problems, or it's the place where you can go and talk about your problem. If workers come to the shop steward committee, we go to the supervisor and talk about the problem and solve it.

Loide Kassingo enlarged on this:

> Women join unions as workers. They are oppressed as workers, by race as well as sex, and so they derive benefit from the trade union. All the unions have a policy against sexism. Women are on an equal footing, and things will improve over time.

Women's words, and actions, indicate their commitment to the union movement. In Oranjemund, where all the workers are MUN members because they are all employed by the mining company, Rauna gave her view of the union.

> Most black women in Oranjemund are in the MUN. The union has already achieved a lot. The company is now adhering more to grievance procedures. It used to sack people often on suspicion of stealing diamonds, and this has now stopped because of the MUN. There was also an incident where a busful of workers refused a random search. The company wanted to sack them, but the MUN prevented it.

Cecilia described some of NAPWU's successes and the kind of action that led to them.

> Since we launched the union, the workers in the hospital have gained paid holidays. We have 24 days in the year as leave, and you can also have sick leave if you are ill. But if you are ill maybe for a week, it means problems. We have taken actions, like stayaways and negotiating with the management. We have found that some problems have been solved and some have not been, but we keep on trying.

For some women, however, union activity has led to victimization. Sena, who worked in a meat factory in Windhoek, found that the company did not allow her to fulfil her commitments as a union official.

> I had to lie in order to get time off to go to the COSATU [Congress of South African Trade Unions] congress. I said my child was ill, but I was late back, and when I arrived the management called me in and accused me of lying. I explained to them why I had lied. They sacked me. Then the workers came out on strike, and now the management has agreed to reinstate me after three months.

Sena, supported by her female and male colleagues, was thus able to resist her dismissal. She explained other gains the union had made: 'The union is recognized, and generally the management is OK, although a few individuals are difficult. They don't sack the workers when they strike. But the rate of pay is still low'.

The unions' successes have, in some cases, extended to obtaining paid maternity leave. Amelia, also a member of Oranjemund MUN, told how, 'Originally women had to resign if they got pregnant, but that changed, in about 1984. Now they get leave if they have worked for two years, for three weeks before the birth and three months afterwards'.

But Oranjemund seems to have been an exception. According to Barnabas Tjizu,

> Sackings due to pregnancy happen everywhere in Namibia. The unions included the demand for maternity leave in their May Day release [in 1988]. At present we would be happy with one month's paid and one month's unpaid leave, unlike COSATU which is demanding six months' paid leave.

Loide, however, pointed out that 'There is no campaign for maternity leave or social services within the unions as yet. It will be the first priority next year'.

Cecilia's experience in NAPWU illustrates the problems encountered when the unions try to take up the issue.

> We don't get paid maternity leave. When you are on maternity leave, you don't have money. When we are talking to the management about it, the problem is that they say that maternity leave is a health matter. It's between you and men, so it's not their problem.

She also explained that although women contribute to and benefit from the union movement, the picture has a negative side.

> There are a lot of women in the union [NAPWU], but they are not as tough as the men. They have problems because they stay at home in the evening, and don't think it's necessary to attend all the meetings, like meetings in the evening and so on. If a woman is in the shop steward committee in a certain department, she won't want to attend all the meetings. Here we have a lot of work to do, for instance, the executive committee has meetings every Tuesday from 7pm up till perhaps midnight. And you also need to go to other countries to represent your union, and also to go and organize in the

other regions. So they have problems. They're not free to do things because of their families.

The presence of men at union meetings can also be an inhibiting influence. According to Amelia:

> Women are in a minority in the union, so we don't take part in speeches and so on. We have problems with participation in public meetings. We need to know how to ask questions, and we need knowledge. It's difficult to participate in meetings because of childcare etc. . . . There are no women on the [union] committee [but] women can and do speak out at public meetings despite the things which stand in their way.

The male trade union leadership is aware of the problems experienced by women.

> Women are active in the unions, but not as much as men [said Barnabas Tjizu]. This is because of the larger numbers of men, their 'natural dominance' and the fact that women feel insecure in their company. There is also the fact that women have most of the household duties and, particularly in the North, that they are often not allowed to get higher education. The biggest factor against them is that they are in a minority within the union.

The divisive policies of the colonial government have also restricted women's participation in the unions. Cecilia explained how women had been dissuaded from joining NAPWU both on political and economic grounds.

> Here in central region, we have a problem with the nurses. They think that if a person is a member of a union, she is also a member of SWAPO. They think also that it's not necessary to join the public workers' union, where the majority of workers are general workers. One of them told us that, after matric, you are told every day in class that you are a professional and musn't see yourself as a general worker. They think in a capitalist way. They think that if I'm a cleaner. I'm nothing. But in other towns and regions, people are very tough. In the East and South a lot of nurses are NAPWU members. They understand the need to join NAPWU.

That at least part of the union leadership is unhappy with women's secondary place within the unions is illustrated by the consciousness-raising that is taking place. In NAPWU this process has been encouraged by the political leadership.

> At the beginning of this year, [said Cecilia] we started to use a book produced in Zimbabwe about women's struggles in the unions. We told the women that the struggle is not for men only, but for everybody. A lot of

> them have made good progress. But there is a problem because people follow tradition. As we were starting, SWAPO came from outside. They gave us a task to tell the people that it's not necessary for a wife in the home to see to everything in the home, but all the family must do it. If she has a meeting, then the husband should be there, or something like that.

There is, thus, an attempt to counter some of the forces that restrict women's contribution to the workers' movement – a contribution that is invaluable. But two groups of women have fallen outside such employee protection legislation as the South African authorities have made, and, at the time of writing, have yet to be unionized: domestics and farm workers. Steps towards building a union for domestic workers, affiliated to the NUNW, have been taken, and its official formation is expected.

**Domestic workers' union**

Domestic work is one of the few female-dominated sectors in the Namibian economy. Oranjemund, with (at least until 1988) an exclusively male domestic workforce, is an exception, and most of Namibia's white homes are cleaned by black women. In Tsumeb, for instance, male membership of the domestic workers' committee in 1988 stood at 20–30 out of over 200. The domestic workers' union will, therefore, be one catering mainly for women workers' needs.

The exploitation of domestic workers, and their acute vulnerability, were discussed in the previous chapter. Their conditions have the effect of simultaneously making a union very difficult to build, and of creating an urgent necessity for one. Said Eva:

> The industrial relations situation is such that if you have a problem with your employer there is no one who can try and help you. People can try to overcome problems by talking to the boss, but then, the boss may hate the worker, and get rid of her easily.

In 1987, domestics began to form workers' committees, in preparation for starting a union. By August 1989, Loide was able to say that,

> There are committees now in Windhoek, Tsumeb, Swakopmund, Luderitz, Walvis Bay, Keetmanshoop, Okahandja and Otjiwarongo. We hope to organize in the smaller places, too. However, one sector we haven't yet touched is the North, where there are also domestics.

She explained that the union was already popular. 'People are eager to join. They have to lie to their employers in order to get time off to attend seminars.' The enthusiasm of workers in Tsumeb was confirmed by representatives of the committee there in an interview in 1988. 'The union began in January this year. At first there were 187 members, but later it increased to more than 200.' They had started the union, they said, in order to improve their conditions at work.

> We want to be paid more, and we want a basic minimum salary of at least R200 per month. We also want to be paid overtime when we are looking after our employers' children. We want to be paid extra for each skill we have, like washing, ironing and so on. We want to be paid at least R250 per skill, but we don't really expect to get it.

The Tsumeb committee's strategy to achieve its aims began with a demand for contracts.

> We are fighting for our contracts. We must have a written contract with our employers, in which they must state everything: how the worker is going to have her money, and how she's going to be paid if she works overtime, and maternity leave too – when she's on maternity she must also have money. The contract would also be protection against dismissal.

This demand had led to difficulties.

> No employers have signed these contracts yet. The problem is that if they hear that the employee is planning to have a contract, they dismiss her. Three cases of firing people because of this have been reported to the union. There are more, but people are afraid to speak out. . . . It isn't possible to strike, because not all the people can do that. You can't trust some of them. But we do suggest that, if the workers are strong and united, if the employer does something wrong to one of us, then we must all decide not to work for that employer. But we haven't done this yet.

The Tsumeb committee's experience clearly illustrates the problems facing the union in a sector where the workers' isolation gives them less leverage than, for instance, their counterparts in the mines. Industrialization has made it much easier for workers to organize. Loide was also aware of the employers' hostility to the union: 'If they find out one day that an employee is on a workers' committee, then tomorrow they will kick her out.' According to her, most of the committees were not yet as far advanced as that in Tsumeb. 'At present we don't have an active strategy. We are still at the stage of organizing and making people aware of the benefits they will get from a union.'

Domestic workers in Tsumeb stated that their aim was eventually to include agricultural workers in the union, although this had not yet been attempted. But this policy does not appear to have been adopted by the union at large. According to Loide: 'It was not decided that the union should include agricultural workers. We have not yet started with them'. The union was not, however, intended to be for domestics only.

> Our main aim is not to maintain the domestic sector. We are combining domestic workers and income-generating workers (who raise money by cooking food, making dresses, knitting and so on) in the same union. Often domestic workers become income-generating workers, and vice-versa.

Later on we want to introduce the idea of co-operatives.

She was uncertain when the union would be formally constituted, and thought that the length of time taken to do so reflected the difficulty of the exercise rather than the status given to women within the labour movement.

It has taken longer to launch than the other unions because it is not as strong as the others. Some people are even becoming discouraged by the delays. But we hope to launch it in September [1989].

## The development of workers' solidarity

The union movement is not new; it is as old as colonialism and capitalism in Namibia. The first recorded strike was in 1893.[3] Early industrial action (with a few exceptions) usually do not seem to have involved women, but this was because the division of labour enforced by the authorities meant, as explained above, that few women were in paid employment. With the gradual incorporation of women into the waged sector, their participation in solidarity and strikes increased.

Between 1916 and the end of the 1940s workers' protests led to a number of local strikes, mainly in the mines. This period is not well documented, but there are reports of unions existing in Luderitz. More information is available for the 1950s, when there were a number of strikes and go-slows at Luderitz and Walvis Bay, which were met with harsh repression. Worker organization in these towns fed directly into the formation of the Ovamboland People's Organization (OPO) (which, in 1960, became SWAPO).[4] That it did so helps to explain why the unions failed to achieve an independent structure at this stage. Instead, the close links between the political and economic struggles were stressed by workers and OPO officials alike, who were often the same people. Sam Nujoma, later (and still) president of SWAPO, was sacked from his job on the railways for attempting to start a union.[5] His mobilizing work for the OPO, in which he presented it as a workers' organization, in fact emphasized the identification of the industrial and political struggles. 'Will you join the struggle to abolish contract labour?', he asked. Everyone shouted 'Yes! Yes, that's what we want!'.[6]

The level of workers' protests did not diminish after the 1950s. Fifty strikes are recorded for the period between 1950 and 1971, including one by laundry women in Windhoek in about 1956.[7] Not until 1971, however, did the extent of unrest among Namibians force itself on the notice of the white population and the world at large. That year, on 13 December, saw the beginning of a five-week general strike backed by an estimated 13,000 migrants in which domestic and agricultural workers were also involved. Their action, encouraged by the SWAPO Youth League, was partly provoked by South Africa's refusal to withdraw from Namibia, even after the 1971 ruling of the International Court of Justice that its occupation was illegal. The strikers' basic grievances were both economic and political, and again illustrate the close links between the two. Workers demanded the abolition of contract labour, freedom to live with their wives and children, adequate wages, a choice of work, job creation in the 'homelands' and payment on merit, not colour.

Initially, both employers and the authorities greeted the strike with intransigence. Faced with this attitude, the workers returned to their homes in the North, where martial law was imposed and the South African army brought in for the first time.

Eventually some concessions were granted, and work was resumed, although the deal was made through agreement between the bantustan authorities and the 'government', not the workers' leaders. Some regulations were relaxed, and SWANLA (South West Africa Native Labour Association), the body that recruited migrant labourers, was abolished. In the long run, however, these changes proved to be little more than cosmetic and the contract labour system was not ended.[8]

The participation of women in the 1971–72 strike may be inferred from the action taken by domestic workers, although their numbers are unknown and some domestics were men. Perhaps more significant is the support that male strikers must have received from their families. Going home to the bantustans not only meant the loss of cash earnings, but an extra strain on the resources of the farms, where the women were usually responsible for production. The continuation of the strike for more than a month testifies to the strength of the social and family structures. Women were also particularly involved through the strikers' demands that families be allowed to live together.

If the great strike produced few immediate results, its effects were far-reaching. The whites were disillusioned of their assumption that blacks were happy with migrant labour, and the power of industrial action to hit the economy and alarm the authorities had been clearly demonstrated. For black Namibians it was a turning point, leading to intensified action and eventually a structured and organized union movement. White reaction was two-fold. Repression of workers was a standard way of dealing with unrest, whether through summary dismissal or raiding of compounds, much of which could only have been carried out with the active collaboration of the employers and the authorities.[9] But there were also attempts to neutralize or split the workers' movement. One way of doing this was through management's promotion of toothless 'liaison committees' in an attempt to divert the unionists. Another tactic was employed by the SWA Municipal Staff Association in 1978 when, bowing to the inevitable, it admitted 2,000 black workers, but also changed its constitution to prevent blacks out-voting whites.[10]

Women's involvement in unions and strike action seems also to have increased during this period. Women were active participants in the Nama teachers' strike of 1976–77 (because of the high proportion of women working in this profession) which lasted for 74 days, and was an attempt to eliminate the system of salary differentials based on colour; this strike has been called 'the most grimly fought campaign in Namibia since the general strike [of 1971–72]'.[11] In 1982 women at the newly-opened Table Top fish factory in Walvis Bay went on strike and won the right to be paid overtime rates for work done on a public holiday.[12] Women, too, whether living in bantustans or townships, were always called upon for material and moral support when their men went on strike.

**The NUNW, unity and politics**

The formation of the National Union of Namibian Workers (NUNW) in 1977[13] was – strictly speaking – illegal, because a 1953 Ordinance prohibited 'natives' from either joining or forming a trade union. This law was, however, abolished in 1978, although a regulation requiring unions to register with the government was retained in order to give the authorities an effective means of control. Nevertheless, a body with the potential for organizing the trade union movement had been born.[14]

The creation of the NUNW was thus both an end and a beginning. That it was tolerated at all marked the extent to which the authorities had given way to constant pressure from workers, and how far the strategy of repression had failed. And in forming the NUNW, the workers were not only signalling the distance they had travelled, but also how much they meant to gain in the future.

They were also indicating that they saw unity among Namibian workers as essential to achieving their goals. The NUNW's constitution includes 'unity and solidarity among all workers in Namibia' as one of its aims, and also commits the organization to opposing 'all tribalism and ethnic grouping as well as types of discrimination among Namibian workers, and [to] fight for the abolishment of all barriers of estrangement presently existing'.[15] The motivation for unity remains strong. Speaking at a workers' rally on May Day 1988, Erika, representing the SWAPO Women's Council, stressed that 'there is only one way to freedom: unite. Forget the things that divide us. Let us stand together and protect each other against attack from the employers and the racist government'.

Erika also summed up the driving motives for union activity, as well as the necessary relationship between the trade unions and the political situation.

> Why do we live in poverty? Why do we have no rights? Why do we work so hard for low wages? Because we are the workers of the world. Because the employers want to be rich through us. . . . Too many are tricked by the Boers' politics. We have our own politics. All workers want freedom from poverty and oppression and war. We want a better life. Let us fight for a living wage!

In a country where the authorities were so closely involved in repression of worker organization, and where class boundaries reflect so fully the 'government's' apartheid policies, that the trade unions exercise the right to make political statements is inevitable. 'You can't separate the political struggle and the workers' struggle', said Loide Kassingo. A statement against exploitation and apartheid by representatives of all the unions in Tsumeb clearly illustrates this point.

> We are against exploitation, which is committed by the employers . . . we want a living wage for the job we're doing. Secondly, the issue of apartheid. It is in working conditions, and the whole country everywhere. We want it to be ended.

Other demands were for training, proper negotiating channels and the abolition of migrant labour.

The NUNW's political stand is clearly stated by the commitment in its constitution to 'a complete change in the present social, economic and political order'. For this it has paid dearly. In 1978 its affiliation to SWAPO was outlawed when a new proclamation banned links between political parties and trade unions[16], and in 1980 its offices were closed and its assets taken over by the authorities.[17] The union was forced underground until it was resurrected late in 1985.[18]

Its subsequent reconstruction in the teeth of continued repression has been phenomenal. It has become the umbrella under which six new unions have been formed, with, at the time of writing (1988–89), the possibility of a seventh in September 1989. The existing unions are NAFAU (Namibian Food and Allied Union), MUN (Mineworkers' Union of Namibia), NAPWU (Namibian Public Workers' Union), MANWU (Metal and Allied Namibian Workers' Union), NATAU (Namibian Transport and Allied Workers' Union) and NANTU (Namibian National Teachers' Union).

The unions' membership is one indication of their strength. In March 1989, the MUN had 11,160 members and in February of that year NAPWU membership stood at 10,000.[19] In August 1989 NANTU, then only four months old, could boast a membership of well over one-third of the country's teachers.[20] Another such indication is their capacity for strike action. In June 1988 a two-day stoppage by all the unions, in support of students who were on strike in protest at the location of military bases next to their schools, not only brought much of the country's industry to a standstill but also demonstrated the extent to which unity had been achieved.

Success is also evident through the growing number of employers who have signed agreements with local union branches. Of particular significance were the recognition agreements made between two of Namibia's biggest companies – CDM and Rossing – and the MUN in June and November 1988 respectively.[21] Furthermore, the 'government' failed to prevent the unions affiliating to SWAPO.

Repression of the unions continued with the expansion of the NUNW and its affiliates. At the time of writing, they are still compelled to register with the authorities but, for example, NAPWU although formed in 1987, has not yet been permitted to register. Union leaders have been imprisoned and workers sacked because of their union membership, especially when taking action. In August 1987, 4,000 striking miners were dismissed by Tsumeb Corporation Ltd, with considerable help from the police. Nevertheless, the NUNW has consistently forced the authorities further into a corner. This is manifested, in particular, by 1) the authorities' encouragement of non-NUNW trade unions;

and 2) the Wiehahn Commission.

Some of the unions not affiliated to the NUNW are mainly white, such as the staff associations of SWACOL (South West Africa Confederation of Labour). Conversely, the Namibian Trade Union (NTU) has been promoted by the authorities in an attempt to draw black workers away from the NUNW.[22] Barnabas Tjizu was scathing about the 'puppet unions':

> There are unions for domestic, transport, automobile, farm and public workers under the umbrella of the NTU. There is also a building workers' union with backing from the "government". When there are disputes, the authorities intervene and settle them. The NTU has offices in a "government" building. The ordinary workers can't get access, so they end up coming to the NUNW. There is ignorance among workers about the unions. Some are deceived by people claiming to be from NUNW unions and selling membership cards on the street. Real unions organize only through workers' committees at the workplace.

Cecilia Paulus explained how the authorities were attempting to undermine union organization among public sector workers.

> We have a problem, which is that we are not yet registered. The government said that it's not necessary to be a member of a union, because they have another association. The government doesn't want us to be in a union. We have a problem with the government, and the members of government are our employers too.

The appointment of Professor Nic Wiehahn in November 1987 to head a Commission to review the labour laws was another signal of the unions' success. Wiehahn had been responsible for labour control strategies in South Africa, and apparently the authorities in Namibia also now saw the need for such measures. With no union representative sitting on the Commission, the exercise was reminiscent of tactics employed in the 1972 strike. Despite having no confidence in the Commission, the unions, nevertheless, challenged it with their minimum demands, including union recognition and the right to strike. The general tendency of the various measures proposed by the Commission in June 1989 appeared to be to give workers a certain number of rights while preserving the employers' control. Whether the new government will find the report useful, in part or in whole, remains to be seen.[23]

**Looking to independence**

In August 1989, in the middle of the election campaign, women trade unionists were looking forward and discussing their hopes for the workers' movement after independence, and how women might be affected.

> We are hoping that SWAPO will win [said Loide]. SWAPO is a member of the International Labour Organization, and has ratified most of its

conventions – though this is still theoretical because it was done in exile. The ILO conventions include commitment to equal opportunities and education, to fighting against sexism, and also to recognising the family responsibilities of workers. The government must create a favourable climate for women by providing crèches and so on. Another issue is statistics, which at the moment are either wrong or purposely withheld. We hope the new government, and the unions, will take this on. We can't strategize if we don't know the number of women in each sector.

Cecilia, too, had a clear idea of the changes necessary in the unions.

At the moment we are affiliated to SWAPO and all our demands are the same as SWAPO's. It's the same struggle. We are now against South Africa, all of us, and we are trying to mobilize the people and tell them what SWAPO is. But after independence we shall look at how to separate the unions and SWAPO, and make the unions independent. When we are independent I hope that we can take action and make demands.

Both women, therefore, looked forward to a SWAPO victory as an event that would both create the conditions in which workers' rights could be achieved, and which would make the lot of women easier. The chances of the realization of at least some of their hopes seem high, but whatever the victories achieved they will be the result of a hundred years of workers' struggle by both women and men.

# 4. 'Every day we hear the voice of guns'

## Women and health

'Health here in our country is not so good . . . because the war is a very big problem . . . you can sit at home at night and you cannot go to the hospital. You are afraid of the war'. This is how a primary health care worker in the North of Namibia outlined what, both to health workers and others in the area, was the major cause of ill-health: the war and the South African occupation. In addition to those attributable to the war, the main health problems for Namibia's women are the diseases and injuries caused or exacerbated by the poverty in which most of them live, and the inadequacy of the health services.

### Effects of the war

#### Direct effects

Ostensibly, since 1 April 1989, there was no war. The UN Transition Assistance Group, UNTAG was then in the country and the UN plan for the independence of Namibia was underway. Sadly, this brought no improvement in the quality of life, particularly for the people in the North. The intimidation, harassment and destruction of property continued as it had during the war. This fact was tragically underlined by the events on 1 April 1989. While the UN's presence was being celebrated in the capital, Windhoek, in Owambo in the North, 33 SWAPO fighters were massacred as they gathered to hand themselves in to the UN troops. The number of dead increased to 140 over the weekend.

'Koevoet', the most notorious and feared part of the police force, were still at large at the time of writing, intimidating Namibians in an attempt to prevent them supporting SWAPO. Since its inception in 1979, the majority of Koevoet's victims have been ordinary villagers. Accounts of its activities make gruesome reading, as we have seen in chapter one: schoolgirls and elderly women raped; tortures, detention, children burnt or buried alive, raids on hospitals, destruction of whole villages, crops and so on, all form part of the Koevoet's activities. According to Dr Shivute at Oshakati Hospital, the main causes of health problems in the area were the war and the curfew:

> Some people die unnecessarily because of the curfew, because they don't reach the health services in time. Some get shot, injured, maybe killed, while

> trying to reach the health services, and some get shot while just moving about at night. The curfew is unnecessary and should go. . . . Other patients come because of the war. They are shot, usually by the South African army or by Koevoet. They are brought to Oshakati Hospital and we show them to journalists. . . . These are people shot during daylight. Last weekend I had to send a patient very early down to Windhoek Hospital because he was shot in the neck by the Koevoet at Okalongo and had sustained fractures to the vertebrae of the neck.

The curfew was lifted in early 1989 (although reinstated for a time in response to the fighting in April) but the legacy of anxiety, and the social changes it brought about, will remain for some time to come.

Injuries as a result of military activity were numerous and well documented. For example, the following report appeared in *The Namibian* in March 1988:

> Marcelina Silas died after being crushed by a police Casspir while sitting inside a hut at the village of Onawa in the Ombalantu district of Northern Namibia. The tragedy occurred on June 10 1987, when Koevoet troops were supposedly tracking SWAPO guerrillas in the area . . . Last week Mrs Kamulungu, who still lives at Onawa, retold what happened that day.
>
> "I heard shouting nearby. Suddenly this strange man ran into the kraal. I picked up my daughter and ran into the house. Then two Casspir trucks drove through the fence and straight into the house . . . I was still holding my child in my arms when the wheel of a Casspir seized her from me. I screamed and tried to grab Marcelina, but the Casspir had also driven over my legs".
>
> The security force members then drove off, leaving the demolished homestead and dead bodies behind.[1]

Torture was also a common tactic of the military forces. There were repeatedly reports of: beatings, sleep deprivation, burial in holes in the ground, being forced under water, strangulation, suffocation, suspension from poles or ropes, being held over fires, threats of death and being shown corpses, threats with snakes, electric shocks on various parts of the body including genitals, and being held against the hot exhausts of military vehicles.[2] Children were singled out for torture just as much as adults. Erastus Haitengela gives an eye-witness account:

> On April 19 1988, at Oshakati Secondary School, 30 kilometres west of Oluno, also in Northern Namibia, six Koevoet thugs armed with R-5 rifles broke into the girls' dormitory and threatened to shoot them if they resisted.
>
> They raped three schoolgirls. When one of them tried to scream, they fired a few shots on to the floor, and when they had finished, they beat the girls unconscious and left. The girls were taken to the hospital and the incident was reported to the police, but as usual nothing was done to arrest the culprits. Another incident happened in the Oshali area, 10 kilometres

from my home, on May 18 1988. A 39-year-old mother Maria Shapua and her two sons Thomas (aged 12), and Egunda Katope (15) were on their way to visit a relative. They were stopped by a Casspir truck full of Koevoet soldiers who started to ask them about SWAPO guerrillas operating in that area. Two of the soldiers jumped out of the Casspir and went directly to the woman, tore off her clothes and raped her in front of her sons who were by then being beaten by the other soldiers. Afterwards, the soldiers dug a deep hole where they buried the woman and her sons up to their necks. A passer-by came to their rescue. Again the incident was reported to the police but was dismissed allegedly due to lack of evidence.[3]

The physical and psychological effects of such treatment places an impossible burden on an inadequate health service. The hospitals are severely understaffed, and the situation becomes worse as white South African personnel withdraw.

**Indirect effects**

Accurate statistics in Namibia are difficult to obtain. Many births and deaths are not registered as people are unwilling to co-operate with the government's ethnicity classification system. Infant mortality rates are estimated as: 163 per 1,000 live births for 'blacks'; 145 per 1,000 for 'coloureds'; 21.6 per 1,000 for 'whites'. The rate of live births for black infants is well below the average for Africa. The contrast in life expectancy between those classified as whites and blacks is equally marked. For whites life expectancy is between 68 and 72 years, for blacks, between 42 and 52 years.[4]

Debilitating poverty is responsible for widespread ill-health among Namibians. Gastro-enteritis, measles, tuberculosis, parasitic diseases, malaria, typhoid, polio, whooping-cough, eye infections and diphtheria are all endemic. Children are particularly susceptible; gastro-enteritis for example, occurs in 17% of children under five years of age. In 1986, a nutritional survey conducted by Oxfam indicated that over 25% of black children included in the survey were underweight, 10% 'wasted' and 17% 'stunted'. The survey also showed evidence of widespread malnutrition among black children in all three areas of investigation: Katutura (urban), Berseba (southern rural), and Otjimbingue (central rural).[5]

Malnutrition greatly increases children's vulnerability to many diseases. According to the UN Institute for Namibia, meningitis, gastro-enteritis and tuberculosis are approximately 40 times more prevalent in black than in white children.[6] The totally inadequate facilities and health care provision have led to this high incidence of ill-health and also been responsible for the lack of data. For black children there has been no regular system of health surveys, only those cases that reached the hospital are known; and hospital admission limited to the most severe cases. Amongst the white population, however, if a child showed signs of diarrhoea it was admitted directly to hospital. Medical care costs money and, occasionally, parents unable to pay the fees, or to feed and care for their children have been driven to abandon them in desperation; this is a growing problem. In the words of one social worker: 'We're living in a city where women abandon their babies in dustbins. I've come across many cases of this. It is directly caused by poverty, not lack of compassion'.[7]

Among black adults, tuberculosis is the most common disease. Others are high blood pressure, cancer, heart disease and veneral diseases. The incidence of TB is extremely high, even by African standards. The UN Institute for Namibia estimates as many as 500 new cases per 10,000 people every year, with an incidence among black people of up to 50 times that of the white population.[8] This is contrasted with figures in 1980, of 25 per 10,000 in South Africa, where occurrence in the black population was 15 times that of whites.

Tuberculosis, a disease resulting from poverty, overcrowding, bad sanitation and unsafe water supplies, is particularly high among black migrant workers, and commoner in rural than urban areas. A survey in 1984 by the development unit of the CCN in Katutura estimated an incidence as high as 9%.[9] A 1985–86 Mayoral report showed that in Katutura too, 8% of the population were victims of cancer. There is no research and development programme addressing the issue of causes or strategies for improved treatment.

Sexually transmitted disease is one the most common health problems. In Katutura, in 1986, it was said to affect 10% of the population.[10] This problem is linked with the systematic disruption of Namibian families, and the accompanying increase of prostitution and rape, particularly around the military towns. AIDS is obviously a matter of concern, but at present, other life-threatening diseases are more pressing for the under-resourced service. In May 1988, Dr Shivute at Oshakati Hospital reported that there had so far been no cases of AIDS, but was expecting that: 'Soldiers may be the people who will spread the disease, because they are indiscriminate in their sexual behaviour.'

There are facilities for HIV testing at Onandjokwe Hospital, and from a small random blood-testing survey, one woman was found to be positive. Dr Tueumuna at Oshakati described the low level of public information on the subject:

> There have been programmes on the radio from SWABC [South West Africa Broadcasting Corporation] calling it a 'disease of homosexuals'. There is one private pharmacist in the whole area who has condoms. None are available at the hospital, and people don't know what they're for.

Dr Tueumuna said that doctors were very alarmed about AIDS, but had little reliable information; for example they had heard from East Africa that heterosexual non-venereal transmission was being postulated as a cause. She suggested that the way to fight the disease was to fight promiscuity. Apparently, so far, AIDS has made few inroads into Namibia, and people are generally ignorant of its causes and effects. A common attitude in the medical profession has been that it is not a priority because people are dying of so many other diseases, and that encouraging the use of condoms is not a realistic option, mainly because of traditional attitudes to contraception. These attitudes are changing, as is the level of concern about the issue.

High blood pressure is said to be related to high salt and fat consumption, and it occurs most often in areas where the diet regularly includes large quantities of meat. According to Dr Ihuhua from the Otjimbingue people's clinic:

> Hypertension is more common in urban areas. The reasons for it are unclear. Most men are very mobile. They have worked in industry and so on, so most communities are mixed urban and rural experience. It's likely that more men than women suffer from hypertension, but there is no research. . . . It may also be due to the stresses of poverty and overcrowding.

## Living conditions and ill health

The relationship between poverty, bad environmental conditions and ill-health was briefly touched upon earlier, here this theme is considered in greater detail. The same pressures of overcrowding and squalid conditions that Dr Ihuhua suggests may affect the rate of hypertension also lead to a high level of alcohol abuse. It is estimated that 50% of adults in Katutura, and 80% of adults in Khomasdal (the 'coloured' township of Windhoek), are seriously addicted to alcohol.[11] *Tombo*, distilled in the backyards is the cheapest alcohol available. This noxious concoction, is brewed from ingredients such as tobacco and battery acid, and is sold at R1 for ten litres. Children and adults alike are affected:

> Some mothers put Tombo in their babies' bottles to stop them crying from hunger and some children are getting hooked on it. Other children suffer violent abuse as a result of a parent's drunkenness.[12]

Josephine, brought up in Karasberg in the South, describes her experiences as a child:

> Not long after my father died . . . I didn't like it with my mother. Her man hit me when he was drinking, or when he didn't want to go, and when he wanted to sleep with my mother . . . my mother had another man when I was fifteen. This man was the same. When he is drinking he became like a madman and he also hit me. Not every night. He also worked in a shop and did packing.

When Agnes was asked if she had a chance to do her homework, she said:

> Yes, but not all the time because the men brought drink and used to sell it. There were too many people and too much noise. If I went to school and hadn't done the work I was punished by the teacher.

**Economic conditions and social breakdown in the towns**

Sniffing glue and taking mandrax are now also becoming common among children, and a growing population of street children take to hustling, violence, scavenging, prostitution and pimping to survive:

> If one drives from the affluent suburbs of Windhoek to the municipal rubbish dumps just outside the city one is struck by the contrast. Arrive at the rubbish dump and one is met with the frightening picture of children, adults and starving dogs, all anxiously waiting for rubbish to be offloaded so that they can scrabble through the bins in search of food, and in so doing, risking their lives and possibly even facing death. For instance in Oshakati last week, three children died and two are still in a serious condition after picking up food at the rubbish dumps at Oshakati.[13]

Homelessness is an ever-increasing problem, as poverty and overcrowding in the rural areas leads to urban migration. Squatter camps build up around the towns; in 1986 in Katutura an average of 8-11 people occupied each small 45 square metre house. The single quarters, originally built for single male migrant workers, are now occupied by whole families. Anna, who lives in Katutura, described 'rivers of urine' flowing through the single quarters while at the same time people sell food there. For Khomasdal the figures are even higher, with an average of 13 occupants for each house, sometimes rising to 30.[14]

Amenities in these high density townships are inadequate or non-existent. Without water, electricity or proper sewage systems, conditions are hazardous to health. In Katutura, garbage collection is sporadic, and overflowing sewage and rubbish collect on the streets. Unemployment and consequent poverty lead to eviction and the setting up of shanty accommodation, often in others' backyards. But even for this, rent must be paid.

Whole shanty towns have grown up around townships. Thousands of people occupy homes constructed from plastic, tins and wire. Often water is the only service provided. For example in Rehoboth there is a tap for every five or six houses (30 to 60 inhabitants). Ill-health is rampant, and lack of resources on the part of the local administration militates against such preventative measures as improved sanitation.[15]

**Conditions in rural areas**

Conditions in rural areas are equally desperate, as we noted in chapter two. In the North, inadequate conditions were further disrupted by the war (see chapter one). Homesteads are destroyed arbitrarily by the military. In Owambo and Kavango, when a kilometre-wide strip along the border with Angola was 'cleared' of its population to create a military 'free-fire' zone, the displaced people fled to the rapidly growing squatter settlements. The huge influx of exiled Namibians returning prior to the election placed increased demands on the system, but a far more serious problem not yet addressed is the number of people displaced within the country. In the 20 kilometres of shack settlements between Oshakati and Ondangwa, at least 250,000 people live without basic services except for one water pipeline which services the military camps.[16] Over-grazing has led to massive defoliation, and food is scarce; and tuberculosis and other infectious diseases are on the increase. The conditions under which they exist leave people without the reserves to cope with natural disasters such as the 1988 drought and the malaria epidemic.

Dr Shivute of Oshakati Hospital elaborated on the seasonal influence:

> Malnutrition in children is seasonal, although it is endemic here. The increase starts in March and goes on until September or October which is the dry season. The problem has increased in the last two years because of the drought, and also because people are migrating to the urban areas because of the war. Also Angolan refugees have come here. No mortality figures are available; research is impossible because of the war.
>
> In the past, malnutrition rates increased between October and May, because people used to finish the *mahangu* [millet, the staple food]. The new trend is worrying. They are not sure what is happening and are doing a survey to find out the reasons. It is a serious problem, and the drought has got worse in the last two years.

Similar conditions apply to workers in the commercial ranching areas, where black farm labourers and their families live on the farms, wholly dependent on their white employers. A church worker, running a hostel for farm children, said they were:

> No better than slaves. People can hardly survive on the low pay and as a result many of the children we look after at the hostel come to us suffering from malnutrition. The children grow up under a system of oppression and don't know anything else but a life of poverty.[17]

**Mental health**

Predictably, there are no statistics assessing the extent of mental illness in Namibia. There is some provision for treatment in the Windhoek Psychiatric Hospital, if the disturbance is extreme – that is, violent. The effects of war and intimidation, of being forced to exist in constant fear of violence and of destitution, are taking their toll. Stress-related conditions, such as palpitations, headaches, faintness and anxiety are common. Many women have been living in a state of constant insecurity, moving from house to house, between towns and rural areas. One study in Katutura reported that it was generally correct to describe life there as traumatic, especially for the children who experienced 'terrifying nightmares'.[18]

Conditions in the compounds for migrant workers have been equally damaging psychologically. Overcrowded, single-sex accommodation, sometimes with ten or more occupants to a room; sealed-off compounds patrolled by armed police, were conditions that sometimes provoked violent confrontation.

In the North, where experience of the war has been more direct, Dr Shivute noted that 'the delusion of persecution is a common one among a lot of other types of illnesses, especially because of anxiety and neuroses.' It is difficult for those who have not experienced the atmosphere constantly present in conditions of imminent threat of war, to conceive fully the assault on nerves and spirit. Lydia, a trainee on the community health workers course at Anamulenge, near the Angolan border, conveys something of this experience:

> Every day we hear the voice of guns. . . . We see the casspirs go around the houses and go to the war, and stories of landmines on the radio always. In our village we are near the camp. We are afraid.

Wilhelmina Shikomba at the Lutheran Women's office said that:

> Most of the women are sick because of the problems. They have high blood pressure because of worrying so hard. Problems of their children leaving the country; problems of the people who are just missing, they don't know whether they have crossed the border or are killed here or – they don't know. . . . They said they want to know how to help with problems in their family.

This led to a request for some instruction on basic psychology.

War trauma and psychological damage resulting from torture and the constant, intense levels of anxiety and fear have affected the Namibian people deeply, both those in Namibia and recently returned exiles. The problems thus generated must be addressed seriously and on a large scale when the health service for an independent Namibia is being planned.

## Health services

### State services

The pattern of ill-health and deprivation in Namibia is obviously that of an underdeveloped country, but the health services are geared to the needs of an affluent 'Western' population. The medical system is operated on a curative rather than preventative basis. The apartheid system has generated separate provision for 'whites', for 'coloureds' and for 'blacks'.

Comprehensive health care is available only for those classified as white, and provision is weighted towards the towns. Only 20% of the doctors in Namibia practise in rural areas, where 70% of the population live; the doctor/patient ratio in these areas is 1:26,000. Similarly, less than 20% of health resources are spent in the 'homelands', reflecting the white urban bias of the health services.[19] This is a result of apartheid policy that separate administrations, based on 'ethnic' groups, should be responsible for the health service in their area. In common with the education services, this system weights the provision heavily in favour of the more affluent group. In fact, by 1984 the 'white' administration was running all but three of the health services on a contractual basis.

Dr Tueumuna spoke of the desperate problems due to understaffing at Oshakati:

> There are about 15 doctors in the hospital, and there are supposed to be 800 beds, but there are many more patients than that. Children sleep three to a cot and there are beds in the corridors. There are official programmes of primary health care, using registered nurses, but this does not work because there are not enough nurses . . . they are overloaded with curative work at the clinic.

In addition, the hospital sees 4,000-5,000 out-patients daily. The service has been severely reduced as a result of the war, as Dr Solly Amadhila recounts:

> I am mostly involved in health care delivery in the northern part of the country, but I do not think that there is much difference as far as other regions are concerned.
>
> Before the war situation in the north escalated, there was a reasonable amount of clinics operating. These clinics delivered basic health care, including immunization, delivery of babies, treatment of minor ailments. The escalation of the war has brought about a state of virtual collapse in this health delivery, which has led to: babies delivered at home resulting in an increase in brain damage and subsequent cerebral palsy; *tetanus neonatorum* as a result of septic umbilicus stump care; increased maternal death; and an increase in the incidence of whooping-cough and malaria.[20]

Those black Namibians near to medical services often find it impossible to meet the fees payable for these services. Reportedly, in 1986 some doctors in Katutura were asking R31 for a consultation (officially, clinic fees were R1.50).[21] One old-age pensioner, living within reach of a local hospital in Tsumeb described her experience of the health service:

> I have diabetes. I am one of the people who is suffering because of that and so I can't go out and work for myself. I must just stay here, and my pension [R65 a month] is my only income.
>
> I am taking my treatment myself. When I go to the hospital they give me tablets and a syringe every time, and I use it, but it only lasts for one month, and I have to pay R1.30. Sometimes I even ask the people there to give me two, because I can't come out, but they refuse to give me more. So sometimes I don't get enough insulin for a month, so then I have to go back again.

Often, the state health services reflect the regime's repressive nature. Until 1986, health services in the North were progressively militarized resulting in the majority of staff being army personnel with a colonel as director of medical services. This was part of the government's campaign to win the 'hearts and minds' of the people, to influence them against supporting SWAPO. 'That was a crime', said one health worker. 'An injury by soldiers shouldn't be treated by soldiers'. In 1986, the Owambo administration objected, and army personnel were withdrawn. This, however, left a severely under-resourced administration to provide a service. In addition, it is clear from the numerous reports, that hospitals and clinics have been the calculated objects of armed attack, with patients and staff attacked, detained and subjected to harassment and torture by the military forces:

> A woman was killed, while two others were seriously injured last Sunday night following a brutal attack by members of the South African Security forces on outpatients and visitors at the Ombalantu Hospital, in Northern Namibia. One of the injured women, Mrs Veronica Aukongo, 29, of Omulukila was nine months pregnant, and sources at the Kamhaku Hospital, Ombalantu, confirmed that she was shot in the stomach, causing the death of her unborn baby.[22]

Such attacks have resulted in the decimation of the health service. In addition, civilian staff have been withdrawn from state facilities, and many independent, church-run clinics and hospitals have been forcibly closed by the authorities.

Many of the prevalent diseases could be controlled by an adequate vaccination system, but so under-resourced is the clinic system that does exist that even vaccination is rarely provided. There are insufficient clinics to reach all the areas. Where distances are great, or in emergencies, people run severe risks if they travel during the dusk to dawn curfew; it is not unusual for people to be shot on sight whilst seeking urgent medical attention. Often, clinics may operate only one day a fortnight, and then so great are the numbers for treatment that it is impossible to give each one adequate attention. Where vaccinations are provided, the lack of refrigeration in the transport vehicle often renders them useless.

Within the state service, however, there are pockets of good health care provision, because committed Namibian nurses and doctors find they have no alternative but to work within the state institutions, and they are attempting to bring about change. The nurse in charge of the state clinic at Ohangwena, near the border with Angola, runs a health education class once a week when mothers bring their babies for inoculation. At Oshakati Hospital Dr Tueumuna is hoping to start a primary health care programme with outside funding, while Dr Shivute has been involved in setting up first aid courses in co-operation with the Lutheran Women's Office. Such courses are important because of the scarcity of qualified medical staff and of the need to deal with emergencies during the curfew. Dr Shivute explained that the courses cover first aid and general hygiene.

> Participants are ordinary members of the community . . . mostly women. They would have first contact with injured persons, and would go out to teach communities. . . . Some women are taught about delivery of babies,

> and traditional midwives are invited to be part of the group. We want them to learn the hygiene part of delivery, as a broadening of their skills. Traditional midwifery is practised by elderly women who have had children, and therefore gain a sound basis of skills.

One aspect of primary health care which tends to be neglected is family planning. 'I may be old-fashioned', said Dr Shivute, 'but I don't favour it, especially in marriage. We are losing people because of the war and therefore need to reproduce'.

This is not simply a male doctor's attitude. Contraception, especially the notorious Depo-Provera has been used by nervous white rulers to enforce population control on the black majority. The ill-effects of this drug for the women concerned are well-documented, including excessive bleeding, excessive weight gain, possibly also high blood pressure and heart disease. It also is known to cause liver and brain tumours to infants exposed to it through the mother's milk. Use of this drug has been seen as part of a colonial government's war against the Namibian people, in order to limit the black population already severely diminished by the high rate of infant mortality and the war.

Many women of child-bearing age are not producing so many children, as a result of being in active combat. For these reasons a strong sense of resistance to the regime has moved women to organize and resist this and other forms of contraception. Lindy Kazombaue of Namibia Women's Voice, which has launched a high-profile campaign against the use of Depo-Provera explains:

> It is still the main family planning method used by the state. It is only used on black women [including 'coloureds']. There is no discussion, and very high amounts are given to Namibian women; that is 450mg for six months. Schoolgirls are injected without consent; women are forced to take Depo after having a baby, and it is given to the baby through the mother's milk. It is also given to psychiatric and TB patients. Sterilization without consent also occurs, and it is possible that doctors force women to have abortions.

This is corroborated by other reports:

> It is clear from many interviews with women that Katutura Hospital, which serves the black township near Windhoek, frequently gives injections immediately after childbirth, often without the woman's knowledge or consent. . . . Even young girls thirteen and fourteen years old are being given Northisterone in 200ml dosages without parental consent. In 1984, one of the high-school principals in Katutura township lined up the girls due to take matriculation and told them that they would not be entered for the exam unless they had contraceptive injections . . .
>
> One of the leading supermarkets in Windhoek insists, as a condition of employment, that all female employees have Depo-Provera injections.[23]

Family planning is, therefore, a delicate issue because of its political implications as well as traditional attitudes. At Oshakati hospital – where Depo was banned in 1986 – Dr Tueumuna spoke of her approach to contraception:

> Family planning is unpopular because it has been abused. It is seen as encouraging sex out of marriage.
>
> I am getting more optimistic about a changing attitude to male responsibility. I have a private part-time practice, and talk to both women and men. I get a good response from men on family planning and promiscuity, and they seem to limit their sexual activity as a result. Men are now also coming to the ante-natal clinic, and a few are attending the birth.

**Non-state services**

Due to Namibia's political situation, there has not been a large influx of aid from overseas. Non-state health services, mainly large hospitals and clinics, are run by the churches, particularly the Catholics and Lutherans. Most of these were established several decades ago, and thus tend to suffer from the imposition of the European ideology of a curative model. Despite this, however, they have been under constant threat from the authorities and some have been forced to close down. One notable example is the hospital at Odibo, run by the Anglican church, which was attacked and destroyed by, it was believed, army vehicles. The remaining establishments are steadily being starved of resources and, as recent visits to Onandjokwe, a well-established Lutheran-run church in the North, and to Oshakati have witnessed, this process continued throughout the run-up to elections. Toos van Helvoort, a Catholic health worker describes the situation for some of these hospitals:

> The Catholic hospitals were the first under attack, now the Lutherans also come under attack and are experiencing problems. . . . I was matron of Swakopmund hospital until the government took it over. The Dutch government went to Pretoria about it, but they were told to address the Windhoek administration, and the Dutch government doesn't recognize Windhoek. The salaries in the independent hospitals are lower than in the state hospitals, because the state only partly subsidises. Shortly after Swakopmund closed, the Kavango government said they wouldn't pay the subsidy. The Catholic Church threatened to close down everything in Kavango if the government didn't contribute. Owambo still subsidises, but now medicines have been cut. This is very serious, as 50% of the patients are malaria cases.

One exception to the European curative pattern is the recent (1987) establishment of a community primary health care project by the Catholic Church at Anamulenge, in the North-West, about 60 kilometres from the Angolan border. The project was started as a result of a survey undertaken by the Catholic Church, which concluded that the need in the rural areas was not for curative hospital provision but a lay primary health care programme. The aim is to prevent many of the most common diseases through health and hygiene education – thus saving valuable hospital resources – and to train lay health workers in basic first aid and treatment for which the sophisticated resources of a hospital or clinic are unnecessary – for example malnutrition. This project is entirely geared towards encouraging self-reliance among local people, and the aim is to train a rural health worker for each village involved. Its principles and practice were explained by Toos van Helvoort, the Dutch co-ordinator of the project.

> The pilot project will be finished in ten weeks. It started nine months ago. I lived here for three months to learn about the area and talk about the project and about a lay health course. I visited Kamaku state hospital, and their clinics. They were very co-operative, and promised me two nurses. Oshakati Hospital also agreed to co-operate.
>
> Twenty women were selected from this area – a 10km radius from Anamulenge – so that they can walk here. After this, we will move to Nakayale [a new village], and again recruit from a circle of 10km. After that we will start in Engolo or Mahanene, where the clinic was closed because the Koevoet stationed a camp just close by. . . . At the end of next year we will have 150 community health workers in this area. In May 1989 I will move on to Kavango to start the same training programme there.

Volunteers were invited from all the villages in the area, and the course started with 16 women including three traditional birth attendants. Two qualified nurses from the local hospital help with the translation, and will later help with the training. Lydia is one of the students on the project: 'A message was sent to my village that there would be a course and it was announced in church. I felt it was good, and I wanted to start the course because it could help the community.'

Toos uses a participative approach and starts the course with two-day awareness training in which the women express their expectations, their fears and their priorities for what they want to learn from the course:

> They have no salaries, and receive no food here. They get nothing from me apart from training. They come every day of the course. I asked them how many days they would come. They said three days a week. So we said it would take ten weeks. Normally it takes 30 days – six weeks of five days. Then they will continue two days a month for six months. They learn what it means to be a community health worker.

These trainees gave as their priorities: how to deal with diarrhoea, measles, women's illnesses, pregnancy and problems that occur particularly during the curfew, TB, worms, first aid, gun wounds and other problems with the war, alcoholism, schoolgirl pregnancies, unemployment, bad childcare and so on. Toos explained that:

> I teach through problem-solving methods and use role plays, discussion

groups, story telling and discussing narrative pictures. Students also have to do research and give a talk to the group about a disease of their choice. I always ask what the local treatment is.

We evaluate the scheme at every stage. . . . The students write down everything they do, who came to them etc. At the moment, they are not allowed to make diagnoses. They can treat diarrhoea, wounds and so on, but not diagnose TB or pneumonia and so on. They must know when to advise people to go to hospital. Women are afraid to go to hospital, so the community workers will go with them.

The course is demanding. Trainees must show great commitment as they must all fit it into their otherwise busy lives, and it requires skills that many of them have not previously approached:

There is a research part of the course. They must each visit five houses, and must write down how many men, women, and children there are and what ages. They did this perfectly. Then there is the observation stage where they must visit again and observe the health and environment. They have books to write it all in. Then they must give a health talk to the group on a disease or problem of their own choice.

Teaching materials used are posters illustrating various diseases, flannel graphs and many others, but for all her teaching aids Toos is trying to find substitutes using local materials, so that the project is not dependent on materials from overseas:

At the end of the course they get a test – they said they wanted a test. Then everybody gets a first aid box. These are made in Dobra, the materials requested from the government health department, but they haven't yet shown their support.

The women are very keen to learn, particularly about pregnancy, childbirth, anatomy and physiology for example, as for most of them it is the first time they have understood how conception and pregnancy works. The empowering nature of the work is reflected in the way in which the learning is immediately transferred to the other women in the villages, and is already being put into practice, as Aune, a student describes: 'Every day when I come back from the course, the women come to my home and ask me what I have learnt that day'. Lydia, another student said: 'I always go to my neighbours and tell them how to prevent diseases and how they are spread. They understand, and they want me to tell them every day'.

Aune explains that she wanted to be a health worker because:

I want to help the people in my community so that they can help themselves take care of the illnesses, because the common illnesses in our community do not need hospital. . . . They must learn so that they take the children to

> hospital so that they can get immunization to prevent whooping-cough, measles and so on. I am very happy doing this because my community likes to ask me about illness. First when somebody doesn't go to hospital, first she comes to my home and asks what illness she or her child has. And then if she does have this illness, I tell her to do this and this so that she can care for it herself. Or if she has this other illness, I can tell her to go to the hospital to get treatment there.
>
> When I talk to the people about health, I talk to the women. The men do not have much chance to come.

Toos is also sensitive to the traditionally subordinate role that women hold in relation to men, and made the decision not to invite men along to participate in sessions on alcoholism, for example, 'because it would restrict the women'.

This lay system of community health care may well serve as a model for future primary health care systems in Namibia. For a long time in the church-run services, as in the state-run service, primary health care has not been a priority and certainly not involved lay workers. However, there have been cases where local people have taken action themselves and forced a change in the service. One such is the Otjimbingue People's Clinic, which was started by the local people in March 1987. Dr Ihuhua of the clinic describes what happened:

> There was a state clinic, but the ambulance wouldn't go out. There was no medication, the staff were uncooperative and uncaring. They saw forty patients in an hour. There were no proper examinations.
>
> So the people all gathered and marched to the clinic to protest. Then we approached the CCN [Council of Churches in Namibia] and they agreed to fund a clinic and an ambulance for one year as a temporary measure until such time as the state provision improved. After a year it was renewed and is now permanent.

Already the area has seen improvements both in the health of the population and in the service:

> The child death rate is less than last year, and many chronic diseases have decreased. TB is less of a problem now, as is measles. . . . Today in two hours, 14 patients were seen, seven for tooth extraction, two for hypertension. All pregnant women are initially seen by a doctor. There are two permanent staff nurses, and a visiting doctor once fortnightly. There is an ambulance on call 24 hours a day and takes advice on whether to transport to Windhoek or not.

The clinic was set up on the community's initiative and the philosophy of community involvement is maintained. The nurses live in and involve themselves in the community and engage in preventative education in the 'out clinics'.

The clinic is an amazing testament to the real desire for the single women left

> on this reservation to improve the care of the whole community including their children. It has lifted the health role into an everyday activity for the community. People are so much more aware here.[24]

It is a tribute to the Council of Churches in Namibia that they have seen fit to resource this project – providing staff and other resources. Perhaps because this is a newer body than the churches that belong to it, it has been able to take a more progressive attitude towards health from the beginning. Another example of this is the initiative taken by the health desk at the CCN, which has established Health and Welfare Committees in various towns. The Committees reflect CCN's policy of encouraging self-determination by the community. They operate with financial and other support from CCN, but must be elected by local people and are self-running. CCN requires them to present progress reports, to consult and make collective decisions with the local community and to establish projects that will become self-financing.

The Committee at Dordabis, South of Windhoek, consisting of six elected representatives from a community of 230, has identified its main health problem as lack of basic nutrition, as the people are too poor to buy the right food. Using CCN funds, they have set up a chicken farm, which now provides meat and eggs for the local people as well as having become self-financing.

The Committee identified the main problems for 1988–89 as childcare, as most of the mothers are working; the unreliability and low level of pensions for the elderly; the current malaria epidemic; and the local clinic's inadequacy. In response, they plan to set up a kindergarten.

Such initiatives, encouraging self-reliance and working from a broad definition of health care, bring real benefits for those involved. The CCN, under its Community Development Unit has a water provision scheme, whereby it helps communities with boring equipment and monopumps if the water level is too low for handpumps. To ensure community responsibility, the water must be accessible to the whole of the community involved, and they must pay one-third of the cost of the operation.

For drought relief, it is less easy to adhere to the principle of community involvement, perhaps because the nature of relief is its application in situations in which people have become less able to be self-reliant; but the CCN here also works through local 'Co-ordinating Committees'. Women form the majority of the population in these rural areas, thus community involvement can serve the dual purpose of advancement for women as well as the relief of poverty and drought. At Dordabis, for example, women are in the majority on the committee, and are recognized as leaders and for their skills; they also gain new skills, such as in communication and literacy.

Clearly, a comprehensive strategy for action in the event of drought will be necessary in the future, but it will be even more important for the government to implement plans for rehydration and to begin to repair the damage inflicted on the rural areas by the bantustan policy. The recognition for women that has come from the small-scale initiatives must not be lost in the drive to plan on a large scale. Whether the consultation and responsibility is allowed to remain with the women will be a test of the new regime's commitment to community involvement.

SWAPO's policy in the refugee settlements in Angola and Zambia has been to recognize the vital role played by women and children (as caretakers of their siblings) in the health of the community, and to work with a broad definition of health, on a community health-care model. Lay workers have been trained in preventative health care; to help cope with the psychological trauma of war and displacement, political education is provided to help people understand and come to terms with their experience. The main strategy of SWAPO's health policy, as expressed by Dr Indongo in 1983, is community participation to redirect the 'prevailing racial orientation in health services, as with the curative urban orientation', in order:

> To create an equally distributed service for all Namibians, irrespective of race, sex, colour, religion and social status;
> to emphasize preventive strategy, placing emphasis on the needs of the rural population;
> to supply free medical services for all and to terminate the present exploitative practice.[25]

To put such a policy into practice in Namibia will not be an easy task, but it will be one that any new government in an independent Namibia will have to address, if the inequalities of the present health system are to be tackled. Already, Namibian returnees, both men and women, many of whom are highly qualified, are beginning to take up the challenge. Even though, at the time of writing, there are problems with returnees registering for work, it is to be hoped these difficulties will be overcome, and that the wheels can be set in motion for an urgently needed system of preventative primary health care. In order to avoid creating new inequalities, any new system must give full recognition to the women who have been responsible for the health of their communities in such adverse circumstances.

The politics of health are very hard to ignore in Namibia. Initiatives that encourage self-reliance, and operate from a broad definition of health-care bring real benefits for those involved. But church projects cannot hope to fill the vacuum left by the absence of a properly funded and run state health service. Moreover, the health of black Namibians and particularly of women, has been systematically undermined by the poverty and racism created by the apartheid system. Probably, after independence, progressive church projects will be able to show the way for health-care in Namibia.

Queue for monthly pensions at Ongwediva. Some have walked for three days to get here from their homes

Koichas school: mothers provide essential support by washing and cooking for the pupils

# 5. 'We want to learn'

## Education

Education in Namibia has been characterized by the inequalities that affect society as a whole. For white children, schooling has been free and compulsory; for blacks it has been neither. Only the determination of many black students, and their parents, has enabled them to wrest some kind of education from the under-funded and inadequate state system. This struggle has been even harder for girls, whose educational needs often take second place to those of their male relatives. Nevertheless, a large part of the education system is staffed by and caters for women and girls, and the history of student protest is also their history.

Black students have for years been a focus of opposition to the apartheid system, despite the risk to their schooling. The 1988 schools strike which began in the North in March and spread to most of the country, culminating in a two-day nationwide general strike on 20 and 21 June, was one of their most dramatic actions.

### The schools' strike: 1988

The boycott began at Ohangwena, about 40 kilometres from the border with Angola, where the South Africans had established a base of Koevoet next to Ponhofi Secondary School. During a SWAPO forces' attack on the base, two students were killed in the crossfire in March 1987 and the school students and their parents responded by demanding that the base be removed. This demand went unheeded and a year later, on 17 March 1988, having exhausted other avenues of protest, the 700 pupils came out on strike. Students at Otapi, Eengendjo and Ongha, other schools in the North where bases had been sited near to schools quickly followed suit.[1] Similar action spread through the war zone. By the end of May all the secondary, and a few of the primary schools, were on strike. On 25 May, Anna, a student from Oshakati Secondary School, stated the strikers' case.

> We will not return to school until our demands are met – that is the removal of all military bases from near the schools. The first demand was the removal of the military camp from Ponhofi school, where there have been

> many attacks, and where two children, Albertina Nghikongelwa and Victoria Nghikofa, have been killed. . . .
>
> When no answer came from the military, one other school came out in sympathy. Another base was then established at Ovalombola. . . . The soldiers attacked this school last week with a mortar. The dining room was attacked. Students were not there, although they were present elsewhere in the building. This school had already been thinking about a boycott, and took the decision to come out after the attack.

The authorities' reaction to early protests thus led to an escalation of the boycott. Indeed, throughout the strike neither the Administrator-General nor the cabinet made meaningful concessions, rather shifting the responsibility from one to the other to avoid being forced to make a decision. Nangedo, a student at Ongwediva Teacher Training College, explained the consequences of this hard-line attitude:

> Some students were organized and some not, but all had the feeling they had to go out. Students were frustrated by Pienaar's [the Administrator-General] decision not to remove the bases, and became very angry. This led to the full boycott.

'Full boycott' meant, that by June 1988, there was an action involving 75,000 students and affecting schools in Swakopmund, Windhoek, Katutura, Arandis, Omaruru, Gibeon and other places, whose demands had broadened to include the end of the South African military occupation, as well as the removal of the bases.[2] A ten-year old girl explained that she was boycotting because 'the children striking are my brothers and sisters. We are all children of God'.[3]

Those involved insisted that the students' decision to strike was not as a result of outside interference. A priest at the Catholic mission complex at Dobra, 15 kilometres outside Windhoek, described how the pupils at the school there had suddenly decided to strike on 3 June and had mysteriously managed to arrive in Katutura to join striking students there. He said that the students' decision had been made entirely on their own initiative. 'People are accusing me of transporting them to Katutura. Do they think I can get several hundred children in my car?' And Anna, from Oshakati, stressed that 'we decided to boycott because of our own feelings, and not because we were persuaded by people from Ponhofi'.

The seriousness with which the students' action was taken by the Namibian people is illustrated in the response of the wider community. On 8 June, an emergency meeting in a church in Katutura was attended by 2,000 parents and students, who demanded the removal of the bases. They also appointed a Committee of seven to meet with the Administrator-General. He, however, only offered to move the schools or to build bomb shelters. This intransigence was challenged by the general strike by the unions of 20–21 June 1988 called in support of the students' strike.

The boycott was effectively concluded in July, by a National People's Assembly composed of representatives of the Namibian National Students' Organization (NANSO), parents and workers. On 19 July the Assembly announced that students would return to school at the start of the new term in August for a month, but that their continued attendance was conditional on the removal of the bases. The Assembly also called for the release of all those detained because of the strike, the reinstatement of all those dismissed, the expulsion of racist teachers from schools and of members of Koevoet and the South African Defence Force from all schools, town and villages.[4] The bases were not removed, and some students did come out again, but the solid strike was over.

The boycott had been especially significant for Namibian women – as students, teachers (a profession with a majority of women), and parents. Teachers' part in the strike was condemned in June 1988 by the NANSO leadership when a spokesperson said that the 'teachers have disappointed the students. Some even called in Koevoet at the start of the boycott'. But he did admit that the teachers were cornered by the situation. They did not come out on strike, but sat discussing it in empty schools and many of them expressed support for the students. At Oshakati Secondary School, for instance, they spoke in support of their pupils and called for sanctions against South Africa. Women teachers backed up the demands of their students in other interviews in May 1988, and on one occasion were joined by midwives and midwifery students who were also anxious to show their support.

Women, many of whom had sole parental responsibility for their children, had to watch them take on the force of the state. Many women voiced their deep concern over what was happening as the strike continued. Joyce, a member of the Mothers' Union at Ohangwena, said:

> Our children are at home all the time now. They are beginning to think of going away, making money, joining SWAPO, even joining the army, or going to the slums at the towns to see if they can make money there. It's not good if they are at home for so long. . . . Last month, the women from the Lutheran Church called two women from every parish, and we went to the minister of Owambo[5] and talked about the problems in the schools. We asked him to call his colleagues to speak to us, but the white people didn't come. We want all the women of Owambo to go to the administration in Ondangwa.

That the women's anxieties for their children were well-founded was confirmed by the numbers who crossed the border into Angola and exile as a result of the boycott. Estimates in July suggested that 5,600 children had already left to join SWAPO, and the UN High Commission for Refugees was airlifting them to Luanda, the Angolan capital, where SWAPO was hastily making plans for their education at their school in the Congo and elsewhere.[6]

One reason for this flight into exile was the increasingly repressive tactics with which the authorities accompanied their refusal to accede to the students' demands. For example, Claudia, from Mwashipandeka Secondary School, said:

> The *makakunyas* [security forces] are unsympathetic – beating children in the streets and surrounding students, asking why they are boycotting school and beating them up. Three students from Oshakati were beaten up on their way home on 24 May. At Mwashipandeka, the principal and others intimidated and threatened the students. I was chased away, and there are people standing near the school gates to see if I come there. Some students are still at my school because they were told that the organizer of the boycott is paid by the enemy, the government, in order to destroy the schools.

Claudia's statement illustrates three aspects of the harassment experienced by the students: the propaganda campaign directed against them; the role of the school principals in collaborating with the authorities; and physical intimidation both of female and male students alike. Women were subjected to the additional horror of rape by the soldiers.

Violent break-up of students' meetings was also common throughout the strike. Even before Katutura joined the boycott, its students were assaulted and tear-gassed by police during a mass march on 4 May 1988, Cassinga Day. This was the tenth anniversary of the South Africans' massacre of over 600 Namibian refugees at the Cassinga refugee camp in Angola. Many young people were detained or injured as a result of the 1988 demonstration.

School buildings were also attacked, and in mid-August 18 schools were burnt down. The authorities blamed the students, but circumstantial evidence indicated that, in fact, government forces were responsible.[7] The culmination of the repression was reached with the ironically-named Protection of Fundamental Rights Act, passed by Namibia's National Assembly in August, which imposed a fine of R20,000 or ten years' imprisonment on anyone encouraging another to boycott school or to strike. This Act applied retrospectively and thus allowed for the leaders of the boycott to be arrested. By early September, at least 50 school students were being held under it, and parents gave evidence that they were being mistreated.[8] In February 1989, however, a high court application by NANSO and the unions resulted in the law being scrapped as 'unconstitutional'.[9]

## Underlying causes of the boycott

By their actions the students risked state violence and jeopardized their chances of passing important examinations. Why did Namibian students run such risks and engage in battle against a more powerful enemy?

The answers to these questions spring mainly from the fact that no black Namibian has been able to escape the effects of living under apartheid. The strike was a consequence of the repression young people experienced as a part of daily life, and of the frustration caused by the low level of education available to them. The work of the Namibian National Students' Organization (NANSO) was also important in inspiring and mobilizing them.

**Repression**

The siting of South African military bases next to schools was no accident. Supposedly to protect the students, it was in fact part of a concerted 'hearts and minds' campaign and to dissuade them from supporting SWAPO. Children and teachers were recruited as spies against their colleagues. Sporting activities, camps and visits to military bases were offered, and organizations such as Etango and Ezuva were set up to attract children through such activities and to promote apartheid-defined culture. In addition, uniformed soldiers sometimes doubled as teachers.[10]

As we have seen, the position of the bases often directly endangered the students as the schools were caught in the crossfire during an attack. The bases' presence led to further problems, from everyday sexual harassment of the girls, to military raids on their dormitories. A schoolboy, Erastus, recounted the following incident that occurred a month before his school came out on strike, on 24 May 1988. Local students stressed that such events were the rule rather than the exception.

> On 19 April 1988, at Oshakati Secondary School . . . six Koevoet thugs armed with R-5 rifles went into the girls' dormitory. They crashed down the door of the sleeping room, silencing the girls by saying that if they scream, it would be their end. They raped three schoolgirls and when one of them tried to scream they let off shots on the floor. When they had finished, they beat the girls unconscious and left. The girls were taken to the hospital and the case was reported to the police, but nothing was done to arrest the culprits.[11]

The violence and intimidation experienced by students during the strike was, then, simply an extreme form of what they had had to fear in the normal course of events.

**Bantu education**

The state education system for Namibia's black children has been essentially similar to that in South Africa. A teacher explained:

> Our children in state secondary schools are taught Afrikaans, a little English, their mother tongue, history and Bible studies. With that sort of educational background, you don't qualify for further studies anywhere outside. . . . Many secondary school leavers train here as teachers, and therefore the next generation of students suffer because their teachers don't know science, maths and English.[12]

The figures available on education for black children tell a grim story: overcrowded classrooms, no proper facilities and lack of trained teachers. In

1986–87, in the North, nearly four times more was spent on the education of a white child than that of a black child. Classes of 80-100 are not uncommon for black children, and some schools, such as those in Tsumeb, have to operate separate morning and afternoon sessions because of the large numbers of students. Few teachers in black children's schools are trained; for example, in Owambo in the mid-1980s, eight out of ten teachers were unqualified, and the proportion of untrained teachers was rising.[13] As we have already noted, education for blacks has been neither free nor compulsory (it has been compulsory for white children since 1906)[14] and this has enabled the authorities to avoid the provision of adequate facilities for all. Inevitably, in the face of these conditions, and of levels of poverty that make it difficult to concentrate on studies, there has been a very poor success rate among black students, and the drop-out rate has been high. One survey indicates that one in three black pupils fail to finish their first year of schooling, while 70% of those who reach their final year of primary education fail to go on to secondary school.[15] These figures, of course, do not include those who never attend school.

In 1986–87, the pass rate among those lucky enough to reach secondary education was only 23% of those entering the Standard 8 examination (two years before the final school exams).[16] Only a small proportion of these students could expect to progress to matriculation (Standard 10) and to higher education inside Namibia. In 1986, 104 black students were in technical training at tertiary level. In 1987 the 'Academy', the institution set up by the authorities as Namibia's university, had 3,000 students, but they were mainly at pre-degree level, and only twelve degrees were awarded.[17]

In common with that in South Africa, the organization of the Namibian education system has followed the philosophy expounded in 1954 by the then South African Prime Minister Verwoerd.

> There is no place for the native in the European community above the level of certain forms of labour . . . Until now he has been subjected to a school system which drew him away from his own community and misled him by showing him the green pastures of European society in which he was not allowed to graze . . . When I have control of native education I will reform it so that natives will be taught from childhood to realize that equality with Europeans is not for them . . . People who believe in equality are not desirable teachers for natives.

This thinking was enshrined in South Africa's Bantu Education Act of 1953, and policies based on it were brought into Namibia after the Van Zyl Commission of 1958, by the Education Ordinance of 1962.[18]

Verwoerd's words were not only a classic statement of the reasoning behind apartheid, but also hinted at the white rulers' economic motives for discouraging black education. Black people were to provide the cheap labour that would allow the whites' way of life to continue undisturbed, but were not to receive any material benefits for that labour. This, and the will to control implicit in this kind of education, are well understood by Namibians today. In the opinion of Willem Konjore, principal of the independent school at Koichas:

> The syllabuses used in the government schools are syllabuses designed by our oppressors themselves. They are providing education to a black child to be just reactionary – that the child should just listen and be ready to be sent to do something, follow some orders of some kind.

Further changes in the education system were brought by the report of the Odendaal Commission in 1964, which recommended the division of Namibia into bantustans on the South African model.[19] Minor changes have been made since, but the basic principles remained the same until independence. Schools have been administered separately by the 'ethnic administration', the bantustans' governments, which means for example, a child of the Nama group attends a school run by the Nama administration, and so on. In primary school a child is taught in its mother-tongue, in secondary school, Afrikaans has so far been the medium of instruction – the ruler's language. Thus, apartheid has been exercised through the education system not only through the low level of education provided to black students, but also because it has reinforced South Africa's policy of exacerbating ethnic divisions in order to divide the opposition in Namibia.

Schools have further aided South African domination of Namibia through helping to register young men for the South West Africa Territorial Force (SWATF). Since 1981 conscription has been compulsory for black Namibians, (apart from those in the war zone) and has been another obstacle to obtaining an education, as many male students leave school before they are 16 in order to avoid registering.

The 1988 strike, therefore, was more than simply a minor irritation to the authorities in Namibia. It was an uprising which, with the support of a majority of Namibians, struck directly at the South African occupation. With demands widening to include complaints against the Bantu education system, it challenged one of the key structures in the enforcement of apartheid and of South Africa's domination of Namibia. The authorities therefore retaliated with a heightened level of repression and refused to give ground.

**The role of NANSO**

A particularly threatening aspect of the strike in the authorities' eyes, was that the students were organized in their own union, the Namibian National Students' Organization. NANSO was a powerful force in inspiring and leading the strike,[20] and, together with parents and workers, in deciding what course it should take.

Details of the process by which students made the decision to boycott, and how deeply NANSO representatives were involved, were difficult to ascertain at the time of the strike. Students were reticent on this point, perhaps because they were afraid of giving credence to government propaganda that the strike was the responsibility of 'agitators'. Decisions do, however, seem to have been made at mass meetings, and schoolgirls in the North said that they were aware of NANSO, that there were branches at many schools, and that it was particularly strong at Oshakati Secondary School. They also mentioned that a NANSO representative was present at Ongwediva Teacher Training College when the decision to boycott was made.

The authorities duly attempted to punish NANSO after the strike by indicting its General Secretary, Ignatius Shihwameni, under the Protection of Fundamental Rights Act.[21] NANSO officials were also arrested during the boycott. But this failed to deter further school strikes, the following year, which were called in protest at continued intimidation during the election period. The 1988 boycott had in fact provided the strength, organization and experience for future actions.

NANSO was founded in 1984, to provide a mouthpiece for young people because the SWAPO Youth League, a much older body, had been banned, and also to press for the specific demands of students. The movement now has an active presence in most black secondary schools, as well as in the Academy and the universities in South Africa at which Namibians are studying. Its main goals have been: to achieve free and compulsory education for all; to campaign against the Bantu Education system and for English-medium teaching;[22] to abolish the school prefect system, as prefects have often acted as government spies; to establish democratic Student Representative Councils in schools; to end military conscription; and to campaign for Namibian independence.[23] The work of a local NANSO branch was described by Georgina, the main spokesperson for a group of its members in Tsumeb:

> The branch is four years old, but there aren't many members because parents give the pupils wrong information about NANSO.
>
> We supply speakers when meetings are organized in schools, and we are fighting for Student Representative Councils in schools rather than prefects. There is now English-medium teaching here and in Windhoek for the sub-As [the first year of school] as a result of NANSO pressure. Conscription is another problem. Also, all secondary school children are forced to go to cadets. In the camps, they are indoctrinated that the army is a nice life.

NANSO is aligned with SWAPO and the unions, and at its fourth National Students Congress in June 1988 decided that, 'NANSO is an integral part of the National Liberation Movement, and therefore its ideological-political line must reflect that of the National Liberation Movement, of which SWAPO is the leader'.[24]

There appear to be ambiguous attitudes to the issue of women within NANSO itself. Its leadership is male-dominated, and one leader stated in an interview that he did not think there was inequality between men and women within NANSO. A higher level of consciousness was, however, demonstrated by the resolution on women's participation passed at the 1988 Congress,[25] and NANSO's own emphasis on democratic structures should, in theory at least, make female leadership possible. It was also clear from the interview with

NANSO members in Tsumeb that leadership by girls is a reality in individual branches. Georgina explained that 'there are more women than men in NANSO here. The boys don't care about the struggle. The chairman and vice-chairman are boys, and the secretary and treasurer are girls'.

**Education for girls**

Bantu education has failed all black children, but additionally, inequality between the sexes has meant that girls have come off worse than boys. Agnes Tjongarero, of the YWCA, recalled her schooling:

> There were always more boys than girls. All the hostels are like that. For every girl there were, I would say, ten or more boys. Most of them drop out. There were pregnancies among the girls, or there were failures. My sister, for example, she just decided she didn't want to go to school. After standard 6, she just decided it was not necessary. So now she's around, doing ordinary housework. She got married with four children.

In the absence of detailed studies, the complex reasons for this inequality must to some extent be guesswork. Certainly social attitudes, coupled with poverty, have played a part. Agnes explained:

> Most people, when the child reached standard 6, took it out of school. 'OK, you can now read, go and work and help me with the funds and so on' . . . The first one who reaches standard 6 must leave school and go and look for work to help support the others . . . In the old days, it was a belief that it's not necessary for a girl to be educated – why? After all, she'll get married . . . And with time, things changed, it has changed a lot, it all depends on the parents and their income and so on. Others left school because of pregnancies etc. That happens a lot.

Students at the independent church school in Katima Mulilo stressed the opportunities the school gave because it did not exclude mothers: 'they allow those who are married, with their babies, with their husbands, even if you are engaged, they do not chase you like the government school'.

The career options open to girls are also even more limited than those available to boys. Besides domestic work, other choices are teaching, nursing and secretarial work, and women who manage to break out of this mould are the exception. These restrictions are no coincidence, with big companies leading the way in institutionalized sex discrimination. At Oranjemund, for instance, the Consolidated Diamond Mining company employs women in their own right only as nurses and teachers. Female students interviewed in both Katima and Tsumeb gave the three careers mentioned above as their choices for themselves (although one of them referred in passing to her ambition to own a *shebeen* (illegal drinking shop!). In general, they were thinking in terms of study in Namibia rather than abroad. This was in sharp contrast to five boys in Tsumeb, who mainly wanted to go abroad and study mechanics and engineering.

Some girls, however, (as well as boys) have had an opportunity to escape the limitations of the state education system and to pursue more meaningful studies in the voluntary sector. Most of the alternatives have been provided by the churches.

## Alternatives to the state system

Education outside government institutions has been divided mainly into three categories: church schools (run by individual churches); independent schools (run by the community, with financial help from the Council of Churches in Namibia); and non-formal education (usually also run by CCN). In addition, there are a number of independent kindergartens.

### The legacy of the missionaries

The first formal schools and teacher training colleges for black people in Namibia were established by the mission societies, which arrived during the nineteenth century. With the dual purpose of making converts to Christianity and training blacks for semi-skilled work in the European-directed economy, the education offered by these schools was never intended to rival that available to whites. Sometimes it was wholly inappropriate. A pensioner in Tsumeb said of her experience of education in the 1930s:

> I attended school, but only for five years, because the school only went up to standard 3. It was run by missionaries from the Rhenish mission. I was educated at school in Otjiherero and Afrikaans, although my own language is Nama. I also learnt arithmetic and writing . . . After finishing school, I went to Grootfontein to work for the Germans as a domestic worker.

But Wilhelmina, who, though educated in a missionary school later taught in a state school, had a more positive view of the church's role.

> I went to school at Onamwandi [in the North]. At school I learnt Bible studies, history – including missionaries, and all those European kings, and our national kings also – and mathematics and English. We were taught in Afrikaans, but Bible studies was in our own language, Oshiwambo.
>
> When I started teaching in a government school, in 1966 or 1967, it was a time when the young people began to understand that they were under somebody's yoke. I can remember, at that time the children began to become afraid for the future. At that time the school was under the government. And as I compare, it wasn't like when we were in the missionary school. For instance, the history I learnt was not the same as what I taught. I taught the history of the Europeans, about how the whites came, and how they killed people, and so on. And that is not what we learnt. At school we learnt how to do handwork, how we can polish things and make baskets, and we were really taught how to help ourselves. The way I

was taught was better.

In the eyes of at least some women, therefore, the missionary schools had some advantages over the later state schools. They clearly had a role in providing at least some education to children, particularly in the rural areas, who would otherwise have gone without. Most of the mission schools were either taken over by the state, or denied state subsidies, following the 1962 Education Ordinance.[27] Those schools that survived the takeover, either by continuing to obtain funding from abroad or, in rare cases, by being granted state money, still continue on a slightly ambiguous path, though usually providing a better education than that available through the state. The secondary schools at Döbra and St Mary's Mission, Odibo[28] (Catholic and Anglican respectively), for example, share an almost legendary fame for the contribution they have made to black education. The Anglican St George's School in Windhoek is one of the few schools in Namibia where black and white children are educated together. But Döbra is government-subsidized, and consequently it periodically comes under pressure, which forces it to tread cautiously. Moreover, the fees some church schools have to charge tend to make them exclusive.

Kizito, in Katima Mulilo, a Catholic school with a majority of girls (460) over boys (60), exemplifies a church school that has failed to throw off its colonial heritage. Christine is a white Polish nun who teaches there.

> The girls must pay R60 a term to board, they must buy their own uniform, and pay R5 for medicine, plus R12 each time they take an exam, or R36 to take standard 10 [matriculation]. They can retake each year only four times. There are many failures, partly because of problems with English, the language of instruction; many because of pregnancy; many because they can't afford the fees; and finally because girls don't like to work. They like singing and dancing, not studying.

A former pupil of Kizito described her experience of the school, which illustrates not only the low standards but also the compromises made between church and state.

> I used to walk 4km to school in the morning. The white teachers were soldiers from the army then. They were not good. All the girls wanted to work, but the teachers were bad. There was no maths taught. If you failed you had to take all the subjects again.

**Independent schools**

The negative attitudes prevailing at Kizito – the presumption that black girls are not motivated to study, and the acceptance of failures as inevitable – have been challenged by the work of the new independent schools movement. The CCN[29] School, also in Katima Mulilo, is one such school. It was opened in 1987 to cater for students unable to continue their education in government schools, and offers standards 8 and 10. Most of the students are in their late teens and early twenties. Such is the demand for education that by May 1988 the school had 760 pupils, and their motivation and commitment was made obvious even by a short visit.

Elizabeth, a pupil at the school, explained that she came to attend because 'I failed my standard 8 at my other school because I got a child. So I stayed at home for two years. I decided to come here this year.'

Regina, another student, outlined the reasons for the school's popularity.

> This school is good because we find lessons every day. At the Caprivi Correspondence School [the main alternative for those unable to continue their education in government schools], they only give lectures, and you have to pay R50 for each subject. And at the government school they don't accept you. Here you just pay R10 for enrolment, and then you buy books for yourself, or share them. These books you are not going to give back, but they are yours forever. That's why it's good here at CCN.
>
> So many of the people are just rushing here because it's cheaper, and you get a teacher explaining everything you don't understand. There at the Caprivi Correspondence School, you just go and get lectures and read it at home alone. But here teachers are teaching, and if you don't understand you can ask.
>
> Another reason for coming here is it allows anybody. They don't say, 'no, because you are an adult you can't come here.' You are free here to do everything you want to do.

There are now five independent schools in Namibia, three secondary and two primary. Situated at Berseba, Gibeon, Hoachanas and Koichas (all in the South) as well as Katima, they respresent, as Moses !Omeb of CCN put it, the quest for an education which 'recognizes and respects human dignity and which liberates the mind'.[30] Usually founded out of an urgent need to provide education, the schools have also offered an alternative to the low standards of Bantu education. Koichas Ecumenical Community School, a primary school situated in a semi-desert area 80 kilometres from Keetmanshoop, was founded after the teachers' strike of 1976. The government closed the Catholic school there as a result of the strike, and refused to reopen it unless the principal, Willem Konjore, was dismissed. In response, the community opened an independent school in 1982, with Mr Konjore as its head.

In common with most of the private schools, this school does not use the normal South African syllabus, and also uses English as the medium of instruction. This helps to make possible a more radical approach to education. Miriam, one of the teachers, explained.

> The reason I came here was because I think I have got some light, and I can help my people out of difficulties over teachers. My aim was to teach at a private school where the children are given the right education, where the children are taught that is black and that is white and that is green and that is yellow, not to be taught of a black thing that it is white. In the government

school they are doing that. They are teaching about Jan van Riebeck,[31] and they are not discussing all the issues which should be discussed.

I teach history, and for instance I am doing South African history. I told the children about South African history, and now we are holding a discussion in the class. We are taking this situation in which we are here in Namibia, and the situation in which those South Africans, the Boers, were in 1910, and we are comparing them. The conclusion we find is that the things which they wanted at that time are things we are demanding at present.

In stage 3, I am teaching the history of South-West Africa, but I am also talking to some people here who were in the First World War about how the Boers came in here to South West [when they took over from the Germans in 1915]. We are also consulting newspapers and discussing them.

Another teacher, Sarah, explained her reasons for being at Koichas.

It's not for me a question of not wanting work in a government school. It's that it's better to be away from the Boers. They like to oppress us in everything. So we want to stay away from them to show that we can do things on our own.

She described the confidence given to the pupils by Koichas' more active approach to education.

The children really like it here because they are asking questions. We are doing the same things as in the state schools, but the way we are teaching is different. What they see is that when they were in the state school, they were taught in a certain way, but now they understand the things they were being taught in the state school.

Willem Konjore echoed her statement: 'We feel we have to move towards a syllabus which helps the kids to become self-reliant and independent, working and thinking for themselves'.

The fruits of this emphasis on confidence are evident from a visit to the school, and the girls in particular seem to benefit. Although the issue of sexism is not approached directly, the girls seem confident and ready to speak out in public. Miriam confirmed this impression: 'We encourage both boys and girls to speak out. It seems to be, that the girls are more active than the boys, though they are sometimes shy'.

Similar confidence was apparent among the women students at Katima. In addition to the fact that the school is open to married women and mothers, there seems to be an incipient debate on women's issues. For the school's first anniversary in May 1988, the (mixed sex) drama group staged a play about a man with both a wife and a girl-friend. Discussion with the female students involved made it clear that they were aware of the issues raised by this and were intimately affected by them, although they thought that the boys were probably not open to receiving the play's message.

The involvement of the parents marks another difference between the independent schools and the state schools. Naomi, a governor of the school at Katima and the mother of one of the students said:

> I would never exchange this school. They are deeply involved in the education of the child, in its totality. They take into account religion, and open the lesson with a prayer. If the child is unhappy, they interview and find out the child's background. They visit the home, they keep the parents informed about the welfare of the child. Why don't other schools? I don't know. The CCN teachers are not like other teachers. There is deep devotion. The duller child is not discouraged but built up. They keep the students together to unite and love one another. They work in groups, visit one another, borrow books, worry about one another. Other schools can afford all sorts of things, but there is not togetherness. Sometimes, here, they have to study under trees, but the children feel loved and that pulls them on.

At Koichas, parental involvement is built into the structure of the school. Indeed, it would be impossible to run it without their help, particularly that of the mothers, who take it in turns to wash the children's clothes and to cook. The Principal explained that:

> In the government school, the parents have no say at all. That is not good. Parents are the very first people to be responsible for the children, and they have to be involved in their education. They have to be a part of the decision-making.
>
> We have a management committee which is elected by the parents . . . parents are involved in the education . . . they see how the kids play in the school. They are even hearing how the teachers are teaching in the classroom . . . So the parents, the students and the teachers are working together.

The results achieved by children in the independent schools are a challenge to the state system. Susan, also a teacher at Koichas, said that:

> Most of the children here pass their exams. The pass mark here is 50%, and in government schools I think it's 33.5%. The children go on from here to secondary schools at Gibeon and Dobra. And children who have been in state schools are coming here instead.

In sum, the independent schools have presented an intolerable challenge to the state system, both because of the high standards offered and because of their philosophy, which has not only contradicted the assumptions of black inferiority central to the state system, but has also resulted in direct political education. Miriam, the history teacher at Koichas, said that, 'We are teaching about the present government, the cabinet of South West Africa, Botha and his puppets. So by the time the children leave here they have quite a high level of understanding'. At Katima, many of the teachers are SWAPO members and the school was obviously labelled a SWAPO school by its enemies in an attempt to discredit it. Students (not all of whom support SWAPO) insisted that 'the SWAPO members who are teachers, they do their SWAPO activities at home. When they come to school it is school time. They have to do school work, not SWAPO work'. Perhaps the most significant way that independent school students are politicized is in the general sense of being enabled to recognize their own worth.

The authorities' response to the independent schools movement has been repressive. At Katima, Julia, a student at the CCN school, described the harassment experienced by her husband, who is a teacher there.

> The policemen used to come to our home, getting my husband, taking him to the police station. They asked him a lot of questions. They were saying, 'You are SWAPO people?' So he said, 'No as far as I am concerned I am not a SWAPO member, but I am just a tutor there. This school, it doesn't want people to fight'. Then they said, 'No, you, you are a SWAPO member'. So they can take him.[32]
>
> They want to close the school, so they just try to trouble the teachers, so that teachers will run away from this school, so that students will also not be coming. Other teachers were deported to Zambia. Last year, the police could just come here, saying, 'Oh, we need a teacher so-and-so', and they take him there [the police station], ask him a lot of questions, and then they bring him back.

Another student told how she was harassed and prevented from crossing the military checkpoint at the border of the Caprivi strip going west, because she attended the 'SWAPO school'.

In December 1988, the school buildings at Katima were set on fire by unknown arsonists. On his way to the school to inspect the damage, the founder and Principal, Mr Mwazi, was involved in a car accident. He was taken to the local military hospital, where his arm was unnecessarily amputated without his consent. This is seen locally as an act of revenge for his involvement in the school and with SWAPO.[33]

Koichas, like Katima, has been subject to police harassment. The Principal described how the police came to the school:

> They came here many times, the police as well as the soldiers, making a few turns round the school with planes, casspirs [tanks] and so on, and then disappearing again. So I think, even when they don't come and arrest someone or investigate someone, they still show their presence and try to harass people, frightening people from being here.

But the staff were firm in their defiance; Susan said that the police 'are coming and driving around, but we don't worry. We are actually ignoring them'.

Since none of the independent schools has received state funding, the state has not been able to use this as a sanction against them. It has therefore attempted to establish its control by passing a law requiring all multiracial educational institutions to register with the government Department of National Education.[34] In June 1988, Koichas staff members said that registration was imminent, and expressed fears that this would impose limitations on them. But perhaps the most remarkable fact is that these schools have been allowed to exist at all. Joshua Hoebeb, of the Namibia Literacy Programme, took this as a 'sign that South Africa may be starting to lose its grip'.[35]

The lack of state funding, although it has helped to preserve the schools' freedom, has meant that they all operate with very few resources, particularly because of the emphasis on charging the lowest possible fees in order to ensure that the education is accessible. Teachers have been paid by the Council of Churches in Namibia, but other funding has had to be found elsewhere. At Katima, the school was started in the Principal's house, and he and his wife had to sleep in the kitchen to make room for it. Three wooden huts were later built for classrooms and a staffroom, but these have been burnt down. Mrs Mwazi, a teacher and also the Principal's wife, explained the problems the school was facing.

> Our main problem here is that we have not good buildings. For the first year, we were using our house. And you see too, we have no desks, only chairs. Sometimes we are too many for these rooms and we have to go out, so if it was Monday or Tuesday, you would find us sitting under the tree there.

In 1989 there was some improvement, with the erection of prefabricated buildings. At Koichas, the school has the use of the classrooms of the previous school, but still lacks sufficient space for classrooms or accommodation; the shortage of trained teachers is another problem.

These conditions, however, fail to discourage independent schools' staff and pupils. Their spirit is summed up by students at Berseba, who, despite the fact that they had to work outside in the bitter cold of winter, stressed that 'they would rather have the discomforts at this school than the authoritarian atmosphere and Afrikaans medium of their previous school'.[36]

**Non-formal education**

This is the final main alternative to state education. Its origins lie in the classes that individual churches, particularly ELCIN in the North, began to provide for part-time attenders. Today, the CCN has taken this up and operates many classes, including in the evening, so that workers can attend. There is also an independent literacy campaign, which operates nationwide using literacy promoters to teach classes of adult students. The literacy work of SWAPO women in exile is now being integrated with that in progress at home, and literacy material is being produced in the main Namibian languages. Illiteracy among black adults is estimated to be around 60%; only two-thirds of black primary school leavers are literate.[37]

The demand for non-formal classes is high and they are over-subscribed, particularly among women who are determined to learn. Most literacy teachers are also women. There are a number of reasons why women are in the majority. Their level of education is in general lower than that of men, and in the rural areas they are more numerous. There also appears to be a stronger cultural barrier for men to admit to illiteracy. According to female literacy class members in the Kavango, 'Sometimes, whenever the wife's invited to a literacy class, the husband will just say "oh please, go ahead, I've got a lot of work to do".'[38]

The women explained their motivation for coming to the classes:

> We want to learn how to read and write. For example, now we are approaching the election, and if you don't know how to read and write, you are going to invite somebody to come and do the writing for you, which is not good. Maybe he is going to mark where you don't want.
>
> Another reason is reading the Bible, because in church someone who doesn't know how to read and write is just sitting there while others are reading. And sometimes you want to send a letter to somebody far.
>
> It is very difficult for someone who doesn't know how to read and write to get a job. Also, sometimes somebody is sick. She goes to the hospital and she is told something. She doesn't want just to listen, she wants to read what's been said at the hospital.

Some women experience problems in attending the classes.

> Sometimes, a certain man does not allow his wife to attend lessons. When other women come and ask her to come to the lesson, she will not tell them, 'No, I can't go there because my husband refused', she will just say, something like 'Ah, please go ahead, I cannot go today'. Normally women do not say that they are tied to the house.

**Kindergartens**

One aspect of education in Namibia which has been neglected in most accounts is the few kindergartens that exist. The need for child care facilities for the children of working mothers (the vast majority of black women) is huge, particularly as children do not start school until the age of seven; child care facilities are often one of the major needs expressed by communities. There are no state kindergartens and the voluntary sector, although it cannot hope to fill the gap, is making valiant attempts to respond to this need.

Some kindergartens are run by individual churches. In Katutura there are also two independent ones run by two SWAPO Women's Council leaders, Ida Hoffman and Ida !Ha-eiros. Ida Hoffman founded the community-based Children's World Kindergarten in 1984, where there are now 80 children; the fees are R25 per month. The centre provides not only basic care and nutrition, but also a high standard of pre-school education, including English teaching.

Kindergarten staff are proud of the advantages this gives to the children when they start school.

Ida !Ha-eiros began her kindergarten in 1988, and in May of that year was still trying to overcome the problem of an extreme lack of resources. The fact that 40–50 children attended a kindergarten comprising a bare room with no facilities, illustrates the urgent need for pre-school care. The kindergarten had to be closed temporarily in June, because it was based in premises next to the union offices in Katutura and the children were thus at risk when the offices were raided by the police.

## Education for the future

Education after independence is expected to rectify many of the faults of the current system. In doing this, the new planners will probably look to the examples provided by the voluntary sector in present-day Namibia. As one staff member of the Namibia Literacy Programme put it, 'In a properly independent Namibia, there would be no need for a private organization to be running a national literacy programme, effectively single-handed; it would be one of the government's primary responsibilities.'[39]

The new education system will also be able to take on board the experience of SWAPO in exile. Although it is outside our brief to describe this in detail, in short SWAPO's educational provision to the refugees included: kindergartens and primary schools for all young exiles; a SWAPO secondary school in the Congo; training in administration and other subjects at the UN Institute for Namibia in Lusaka, Zambia (this institution's persistent challenge to the authorities in Namibia led to the establishment of the Academy); an extensive adult literacy programme for the exile settlements in Angola and Zambia; a wide variety of training at institutions all over the world, from primary and secondary schooling on the Island of Youth in Cuba, to undergraduate and post-graduate studies at universities in, for example, Britain, the USA and the USSR.

Finally, the new system will perhaps begin to respond to the demands that women are making. The last word goes to Agnes Tjongarero: 'If you have got a boy and a girl, then the boy must shine. He must get everything, while the girl, she can do the washing, clean the house and so on. It's oppression, isn't it?'

# 6. 'We want our own presidents'

SWAPO Women's Council

In all areas of work, health, education and social position, women have been systematically oppressed, making them the most disadvantaged of all social groups in Namibia. To some extent, as we have seen, in taking on increasing responsibilities, women have begun to challenge this state of affairs and to demand that the struggle to end colonial rule and class oppression incorporates a transformation of women's place in society. But will it? The pervasive nature of women's oppression means that it is easily allocated second place in the overall effort for liberation. The SWAPO Women's Council (SWC) have begun to tackle this issue within the organization, insisting on positions of responsibility and developing the theory and accompanying policy to ensure that women's demands for equality are heard.

## Pre-colonial patriarchy

> 'The generally inferior position of women was perhaps the most systematic social cleavage in pre-colonial Namibian society.'

The term 'pre-colonial', though often perceived more narrowly, refers to societies whose histories cover thousands of years before European colonization; and, while the social position of women varied in different societies:

> In all groups a division of labour operated in which most productive tasks were allocated according to sex . . . The division of labour was least unequal in the San hunting bands, whose skills and tasks were fairly equally apportioned. In the pastoral societies (since livestock were central to their livelihood), the exclusion of women from hunting and most stock-raising severely limited their participation in production and confined them to tasks near the home.[1]

Systems of private ownership allocated most agricultural products and livestock to the men, for whom the custom of polygamy ensured adequate labour to work their land. In mixed farming societies, the produce of separate plots owned by wives and daughters were consumed first, while the male head of household's produce could be retained and disposed of by him as surplus profit.

An analysis by the SWC concluded that men's role allowed them freedom of movement, whereas women's reproductive and childcare roles were more likely to be confined to the home; this division of roles was used to confer an inferior status on women. For example, a Herero woman's tasks (among others) included building and maintenance of the home, and the milking, both of which were crucial to the family as a unit of production and reproduction, but under these circumstances, women were afforded the status of 'semi-serfs'.[2]

## Women's position in present-day Namibia

Women's situation deteriorated sharply with the invasion of a colonialist regime. In legal terms, as Kisiedu of the SWC notes:

> Women are virtually perpetual minors all their lives, with no legal rights. Regardless of their age, of whether they are married or not, women are always subject to the authority of men.[3]

This results from the South African imposition of a system that incorporated the restrictive traditions of earlier times as well as imposing more restriction, so that such rights and safeguards that did exist were abolished. In addition to the legal framework, there are clear social and economic bases for women's subordination, as have been examined in earlier chapters.

The institutions of the state, capitalism and white male superiority share some common interests. More research is needed fully to understand the relations between these systems; here, we do not presume to examine the roots of these relations, but some of their implications must be noted. The all-pervasive patriarchal culture that allocates to black Namibian women the lowest rung on the social ladder is the basis for the hierarchy which confers the highest position on white men, then white women, followed by black men, and, at the bottom of the hierarchy, black women.

This culture is characterized by the maintenance of power through violence, and a white male society. Challenges are not tolerated, and a hierarchical system has been instituted to avoid such challenges. One example is the subordinate male administration in the rural areas, comprising chiefs and headmen paid by the government and constituting a class whose interests are served by maintaining the status quo and the position of male superiority.

In legal terms, the concept of the family also maintains women's subordinate position; technically, they are minors throughout their lives. Ironically, in reality for black Namibians, the family has been devastated by the regime, as people have been forced to live separated lives; the morality of the family is,

Ida !Ha-Eiros of the SWAPO Women's Council

**Erika Ramakhutla of the SWAPO Women's Council**

however, still enforced. The denial of the existence of homosexuality and the perception by many that, according to one doctor it is 'extremely uncommon or non-existent here' is illustrative of this.

Women's reproductive role in the family perpetuates the oppression of women in both the apartheid system and the peasant farming system. Their reproductive role supports the capitalist economy by maintaining and supplying the labour force. It is at the root of women's universal oppression, and transcends national, social, cultural, racial and class differences. It is the only aspect of essential work that, due to its specifically biological nature, requires sexual division of labour. But the biological element in itself is not at the root of oppression, but the use made of it by a male dominated society.[4]

The implication of this is that a simple 'triple oppression' analysis of women's oppression (that is, by race, class and gender) is inadequate in so far as it infers the possibility of treating each aspect separately, and assuming for example, that the gender issue will be solved by political liberation, as is implied in the slogan given at a SWAPO meeting in 1977: 'The participation of women in the struggle will hasten our victory and will thus end the slavery of Namibians.'[5]

Women in the SWC have learnt from the experience of women in other national liberation struggles and those in socialist states that women's position will not necessarily be improved by national liberation. As SWAPO leader Dan Tjongarero explains:

> Post-colonial Mozambique brought reports back that despite sacrifices women had made in combat, they were then forced to revert back to so-called traditional roles. This was incompatible with the new spirit of liberation. We want double liberation on the day of liberation, not after.

It becomes clear by emphasizing the reproductive role of women as the reason why patriarchy has taken hold across the board in all societies, that the gender aspect of oppression must be given priority. Ida Hoffman expressed this forcefully when she addressed a SWAPO Women's rally in April 1988:

> Liberation of women is a prelude and a precondition to victory. The struggle is not between men and women. Nevertheless, we want our own presidents and our own place among the leaders. We want total liberation, not piecemeal reforms. We are part of the leadership.

As a 'prelude and a precondition' to victory, the cultural and ideological aspects of patriarchy must be tackled. In her paper describing SWAPO's position on the integration of women in development Susan Nghidinwa of the SWC explains:

> SWAPO's experience is that institutional frameworks have a limited, if any, capacity to bring about a change in attitudes. There is ample historical evidence, for example, that laws in themselves cannot alter the behaviour of

> citizens. They are just frameworks within which social relations may be created. But the value element should imbue the laws as to give a directive on how the laws should be used and towards what ends.[6]

The women's movement in Namibia has been formed within the context of the national liberation struggle. This has meant that throughout its history the SWAPO Women's Council has been grappling with these questions.

## Women in resistance

Women in Namibia have always been at the forefront of resistance to colonial domination. The forms of resistance have differed according to the specific Namibian context. This context is central to an understanding of how, in practical terms, Namibian women have tackled the different levels of oppression outlined above, and will help to avoid the danger of interpretation in terms of a 'Western'-bound feminism.[7]

In the early years of this century, in defiance of the German extermination orders in 1904–05, Herero women used their specific power as reproducers, and stopped bearing children in support of the armed opposition to German rule. This action also constituted a sex strike in order to put pressure on their men to fight the Germans. They vowed not to bear children until German rule ended in the homeland. The Herero women then led the way in the refusals to work as 'nannies' for the Germans. In 1955, Herero women again took leads in objecting to the apartheid Lutheran church, and formed the independent church, Oruano. Urban women all over Namibia defied the pass laws, and in 1958, it was women who mobilized against the Windhoek Advisory Board, in protest against the Board's application to allow corporal punishment for women pass-law offenders.

Since then, through the wars which followed and the resistance that has continued, survival and maintenance of the family and community in extremely arduous circumstances has been a very real form of resistance for Namibian women. The result of this resistance has not only provided a source of active fighters for PLAN, but by surviving on their own, these women have met the full force of violent repression head on.

In 1959, women led overt resistance to the forced-removal policies of the regime. Notably the demonstration was multiracial, women reaching across the boundaries of colour, defying the divisive policies that were to establish Katutura for the 'blacks' and Khomasdal for the 'coloureds'. The date 10 December is celebrated as Namibian Women's Day. On that day in 1959, the South African forces opened fire, killing twelve people and injuring 54. SWAPO publications tell the story of Kakurukaze Mungunda:

> She was hit by a bullet in the chest; realizing that she had been fatally wounded, Mama Mungunda . . . stumbled, despite profuse bleeding, towards a parked car belonging to the superintendent of the city and

> managed to set it ablaze with a box of matches. Shortly thereafter she died . . . It is a tribute to the bravery and heroism of Kakurukaze Mungunda, that SWAPO has designated 10 December Namibian Women's Day.[8]

Putuse Appollus of the SWC saw in the Windhoek massacre a change in the nature of women's resistance: 'They activated the hitherto patient forces embodied in the indomitable willpower of Namibian women'.[9]

Up to this point, although there had been significant mass mobilization, there had not been such clear evidence that the state would forcibly crush any attempt to challenge it. In April 1960 this led to the formation of SWAPO as a broad-based national organization.

A paper by the SWC presented in a speaking tour of the USA, addresses women's involvement in SWAPO. As a result of the pressure women exerted on the organization, their position has greatly improved and their representation increased:

> At the launching of the armed struggle in 1966, there were only a handful of women in the movement in exile. Within the last 20 years, the women have become visible in practically every aspect of the struggle.[10]

In 1969, SWAPO Women's Council was formed with the task of:

> Not only mobilizing women to participate in the national struggle, but to make them conscious that they have the same right and obligation as men to make decisions concerning their nation's interest; that the woman should therefore develop herself to be a comrade in all aspects and not just a 'homemaker'; that both male and female should understand the system of exploitation and combat it as comrades.[11]

The initial growth of the SWC was among the exiled community, and in January 1980, the first SWC congress was held in Angola. At this meeting demands were made for changes within SWAPO to recognize women's participation in all aspects of the struggle, and to share leadership. In 1976 the SWC was formally inaugurated as a wing of SWAPO with its own constitution and secretariat, and in March 1977, inside Namibia, following a series of meetings, which focussed on the problems facing Namibian women, the first secretary of the SWC within the country was appointed. The women immediately went into action, organizing seminars and rallies. In June of that year, only two and a half months after SWC's inauguration, a women's meeting was held in Walvis Bay, and a week later, a Women's Council rally was held in Katutura, attended by almost 4,000 women and men.

A mark of the strength of the Women's Council is that the women have had such an active presence in the liberation movement inside the country. Characterized by a solid grassroots membership and leadership the council has won mass support among women and has been open and accessible to all women through the appeal to share in the struggle for independence and then to improve women's position. From its beginnings in 1976, SWC has gone on to focus on women's specific oppression and the struggle for equal rights. Much has been done in this area inside Namibia, raising awareness and mobilizing women, and in exile, away from the specific repressive structures that operate there.

## SWC today

By the 1970s, women inside the country had formed effective support networks, holding rallies, addressing meetings, and holding seminars and workshops in order to deepen their political understanding. According to Dan Tjongarero:

> It was a natural consequence. Women were the next group to be mobilized. To become full participants of the struggle. Not only as cooks, nurses, etc., but as politicians and guerrillas. These demands began to be made by the women leaving the country, and was reflected by the women inside. Then an additional dimension was added; that of "double oppression". Women talked of oppression by men also. There was an attempt at sensitizing the men in the liberation struggle. They said "We are prepared to take up the challenge to fight colonization, but are we really equal?"

Inside Namibia, however, the women's leaders were subjected to continuous harassment, arrests, torture and imprisonment, specifically Gertrude Kandanga, Ida !Ha-eiros and others. Ida, who served five years detention after being arrested when seven months pregnant, recounts something of her experience:

> I was arrested on 15 October 1980. I was kept in solitary confinement. . . . A baby boy, Konjeleni Richard, was born on 17 December 1980 but with some complications and he had to be kept in an incubator. They took me to the clinic and there I was kept for three days. When I came back from the clinic I had to continue the work I left behind. I was not strong enough but I tried to continue with the duties of a prisoner which I was compelled to do. If you do not fulfil the requirements of the duties you do not get any food. As a mother who had to breast feed it was important for me to eat.

After 18 months her child was taken away and looked after by her mother, but it died a year later. Ida was not allowed to go to the funeral.[12]

Today, SWC has 27 branches in Namibia, in four regions, with the west and northern regions being most active. There is a central committee, branch secretaries and fieldworkers. Maria Kapere explained: 'There are fieldworkers for SWC who inform women about the political situation. They need training, and the national leaders have been asked to develop a course for full-time workers'. She said that at that stage, in 1988, no separate figures were kept within SWAPO for the numbers of women members; they were planning to keep separate registers. At that time, there was one woman representative on the National Committee of SWAPO.

An indication of the danger that women were risking through active involvement in the SWC was illustrated by the women in Rundu, an area of the North where the military had imposed very repressive practices. The women acted and spoke with extreme caution and in fear of reprisals. This was in the summer of 1988, but still at the time of writing, SWAPO members are conscious that activists put their lives at risk from right-wing vigilantes.

One problem for the women in Namibia was lack of transport, which prevented access to women up and down the country; and too, there was a lack of resources with which to implement plans for development projects. Their present strategy is changing from public rallying to small group work, projects and work on local issues, educational work and so on. In the South, in Oranjemund, transport is a particular problem. Rauna explains that with so few black women:

> It's difficult to meet other groups because of the distances, and transport is so bad. SWC here began mobilizing women in August 1986. We feel cut off, not part of the struggle, not affected by the war. Most of the women come from the North.

It is to be hoped that some of these problems may be solved in the near future now that the SWAPO can be centralized inside the country, and the two wings of the Women's Council – one operating inside Namibia, one in exile – can be integrated.

A consistent concern among the SWC leadership has been the military, and the implications of the war machinery that abuses the reproductive power of women. One aspect of this as Erika Ramakhutla urged at a May Day rally in 1988 is related to women as domestic servants: 'We women are serving the army. Black women are bringing up white children who join the army and beat up the same black women and families.' Another aspect is related to their role as mothers, as Ida Hoffman speaking at another rally said:

> Our sons are snatched away while we are resting. We must begin to assist our sons to resist conscription. Then again if a mother does not care, the son must go forward and resist on his own.

Another concern is that of educating and challenging the men. The meetings are not exclusive to women. 'Women are on the move', said Maria Kapere. 'We must go forward together'. Meanwhile Erika Ramakhutla speaks of the 'double shift' forced on women: 'We women have to work in the white township, and then again we must do the same work at home, while the men relax and put their feet up after work.'

Re-educative work is just as important among the women, as Rauna in Oranjemund, where there is a strong Women's Council group, explains:

> People aren't necessarily politically aware. The aim of SWC is to make them aware. SWC are planning seminars on political awareness for black women. The aim is to get women to discourage their children from going to the army . . . For instance, telling people what 435 is. They discuss subjects from the newspapers and SWAPO information. We want to influence all women white and black. Most of them [white women] only know what's on the T.V. If they were aware, they might discourage their sons from conscription.

Through this work, the women set out to challenge the process of apartheid directly:

> We want to start SWAPO pioneers [children's section]. It is a problem to make children aware, but not to teach them to hate. The little children don't understand discrimination, but the mature ones have more idea. They see blacks living in hostels and so on. They experience racism from other children at school and by prefects. They learn about discrimination quickly. It's difficult to politicize without teaching to hate.

Challenges are also made to their own communities' hierarchical attitudes:

> We must respect each other, men and women. Leaders must respect the person on the street . . . We cannot build a democratic future when women are still oppressed and unable to participate fully in all aspects of society.

It is perhaps symptomatic of women's difficulties in challenging the patriarchal structure in their own communities, that a SWC conference planned in summer 1988 had to be postponed several times due to domestic and child care problems. Clearly, many women are aware of the difficulty of the task they are taking on in confronting the oppressions of race, sex and class, not only in the apartheid regime, but also in the patriarchy of their own community.

## SWC in exile

In the exiled community, women in the SWC have similarly been preparing for sexual equality in an independent Namibia. Much work has been done in developing a theory and policies appropriate to the specific situation of Namibia. Advances have been made in power-sharing between men and women within SWAPO itself, and a concentrated effort has been made in the direction of education and preparation of exiled Namibians to ensure the possibility of a more just society after independence. Susan Nghidinwa, describing the refugee settlement in Zamiba said: 'Our aim is that no woman should be without a job in Namibia'.

To this end, in the refugee settlements in Angola and Zambia, SWC have organized and run literacy classes, education at kindergarten, primary and secondary level, training in food production, agriculture, health education, child care, construction, bore-hole drilling, fabric production and other development education projects. These have been large-scale projects, catering for thousands of inhabitants of the camps. This impressive undertaking has achieved great success. Many women have gone on to further education in UNIN (UN Institute for Namibia) in Lusaka, or elsewhere overseas. It is a measure of the success of the SWC in encouraging women's education that 50% of students completing courses at UNIN have been women. The majority of doctors, medical assistants, midwives and social workers on the settlements have been women, perhaps because women have constituted the major part of the population there (many men were in the army or pursuing further education, being initially better educated).

The Women's Council has also ensured that women have received training in non-traditional vocations such as electrical engineering, law, mechanics and so on. Similarly, women have taken up such non-traditional positions in the camps as tractor-driving, and so on, directly challenging the male traditions in their own community. As a result of this policy to achieve high levels of education and training for women, many highly qualified women have now returned to Namibia, ready to take up salient positions and unlikely to accept unjust treatment on the basis of their sex.

Women were also quickly incorporated into the ranks of PLAN, and many women were trained and served as active combatants in the war of independence. Two members of SWC write:

> In their campaigns of terror on Namibian women, men and children, the racists have driven home to the women the necessity of fighting to secure the survival of their people . . . Where, in the past, women were either victims of attacks or the invisible base of the war effort, women combatants have grown in numbers, and the SWC has provided moral and material support to them. Women commanders in fighting units, political instructors and medical personnel have been a source of pride.[13]

But a tragedy of this long war is that even in the refugee settlements, women were not safe from the South African military. This was violently illustrated when, on 4 May 1978, over 600 inhabitants of the refugee settlement at Kassinga in Southern Angola, mainly women and children, were killed in a surprise attack; many more were wounded. It is commemorated each year by Namibians as a sad memory of the indiscriminate nature of South African military strategy.

## Future challenges for the SWC

Women have made progress in the last two decades, taking them into new spheres and new levels of awareness. It is an exciting time, but have they really taken men with them? Or is it as one SWAPO official said:

> To the majority of men and women inside and outside [Namibia] no progress has been made on the double struggle issues. For men, there is no problem if the women are only wanting parity in the struggle. But reaping equal benefits from liberation? No. Many still argue that women's struggle is a secondary issue.

Of course, attitudes within SWC will vary, and perhaps the theory of the interrelationship of race, class and gender oppression is only now being worked out in practice. In 1987, two women from SWC expressed it as:

> A struggle for national independence, and at the same time a struggle against racial, cultural oppression and dehumanization; against discrimination in all its forms including gender, and for eliminating the exploitation of workers and peasants. Without this comprehensive onslaught on the system, women's liberation can only be partial and incomplete.[14]

The problem of preventing sexual oppression from being forgotten, in favour of other struggles, is something with which the SWC is wrestling. The question of the women's attitudes themselves is understood, as illustrated in a quotation from Martha Ford:

> When one understands how the system, which fosters exploitation, operates and conditions the oppressed to accept their oppressive situation, one will also easily understand what has been the root cause of women being passive objects – trained and geared to please.
>
> We are still male dominated at the National Executive level and at branch level and would like to see a conscious effort at drawing women into the decision-making organs of our organization. We have a long way to go but the struggle will continue.[15]

It is the attitudes of men and women formed by this 'training to please' that need to be changed. Susan Nghidinwa writes that: 'The primary focus should be political education and transformation of attitudes'; and goes on to say, from SWAPO's experience of the limitation of institutional frameworks:

> From its inception, SWAPO created a structure which placed women on an equal footing with men in the movement. The interests and views of women are represented in the Central Committee, the highest policy-making body in SWAPO, and at all other levels. However, it became clear that we would have to have more than the SWAPO constitution and the Party machinery under it, to achieve full participation of women in the struggle for liberation and development . . . We have found that we have to spend inordinately

more time working to transform attitudes without which our formal machinery becomes only window dressing.[16]

SWAPO's official policy is to:

> Accord full and equal rights to women in all aspects of our future democratic society. Their full and unfettered admission to all levels of government responsibility, and to the industrial, commercial, agricultural, scientific, academic and professional life will be defended.

This is an ambitious policy. Not only is it backed up with rights of paid maternity leave and free child care facilities, but a promise to take the initiative in campaigning:

> The campaign to root out discrimination against women will involve not only provisions for equal education, better training and job security for women, but also minimum quotas for their participation in decision-making bodies at all levels of the government, trade unions, political parties, etc.[17]

The policy also provides for a national women's organization to promote the interests of Namibian women. This offers a chance, as to date the SWAPO Women's Council has done, for women to initiate new ways of working, untrammelled by the traditions of male hierarchy, through which they can be seen to contribute new and particular skills and insights. If equality is to be a real possibility, then women's contribution must be seen as the rich gain it has so far proved to be, not merely the result of an obligatory quota system.

It is a measure of the strength of spirit of Namibian women that, during the ongoing effort to achieve national independence they have achieved the respect and status required to produce this policy of radical action. According to Nghidinwa, the transformation of attitudes must still take place within the context of a socialist revolution. On its own however, this is not likely to tackle gender issues adequately. The debate will continue . . .

It is perhaps the peculiar nature of the situation of Namibian women that will enlighten the discussion. In a paper presented at the International Conference in 1984, the SWC argued that:

> It may be that the Namibian family is smashed beyond repair: the nucleus of the mother-child relationship may have to be the starting point of any reconstruction. Black women have been forced to operate autonomously in the absence of men, to bring up their children alone, to take their own decisions, and they may not wish to give up the power they have been forced to take into their own hands.[18]

# 7. 'We want to stand up in Namibia'

## Women's groups

The most widely supported organization in Namibia is the SWC; there are a number of other organizations but these differ from the SWC in their concentration on developmental work, rather than on an overt political approach. But everything has its political implications, and some of the more 'progressive' groups consider that to raise awareness about personal and political problems is integral to their work. At the other end of the spectrum, has been an attempt by the authorities to create right-wing groups to exert their own influence over women.

As we have seen in the previous chapter, overt political activity has been forcibly restricted in Namibia. These alternative groups, however, whether recently formed or of long-standing, have maintained a continuous thread of resistance through the tradition of women meeting together. How the groups address the practical or strategic needs of the women involved, in order to arrive at an understanding of what constitutes 'progressive' within the historical and cultural context of Namibia, rather than relying on a Western, feminist interpretation of progessive development is one consideration dealt with in this chapter.

In the 1980s there was a recognition that development and resistance can be complementary. Because resistance has implications for the development of individuals and the reassessment of their role and status, development in practical terms inasmuch as it empowers people and encourages self-reliance, is therefore itself subversive within the context of an oppressive regime.

### Community development

Grassroots organizing in the community for development is a long-established tradition in Namibia; but with the entry of colonization it took on a different nature. André Strauss, a community organizer in Katutura writes that pre-colonial community organization: 'centred mostly on issues of communal survival in a constant fight to subdue nature'.[1]

With the arrival of the Germans in 1884, the most pressing focus for organizing became active resistance to the colonial regime. This took the form of anti-colonial uprisings, petitioning of international bodies and the rise of national liberation movements. Until recently, the thinking in the liberation movement has been characterized by the tag 'no development before liberation', on the grounds that any development would divert scarce energy and resources away from the main goal: independence. There has been an avoidance of what Amutenya of the Justice and Peace Commission of the Catholic church in Windhoek terms an 'ambulance ministry', which aids the victims of oppression but is vulnerable to the dangers of pacifying the people with immediate benefits, while leaving the root causes of suffering unchanged. Amutenya describes how the church is instead: 'engaged in the ministry of participation in the liberation cause by supporting and encouraging the actions of the oppressed people'.[2] An integral part of this approach is a policy of non-collaboration with the state.

According to Strauss's analysis, due to mass disillusionment at the end of the 1970s, when the high hopes for imminent independence were disappointed, two developments took place in Namibia. One was the growth of a black middle-class elite by a deliberate South African policy of incorporating black people into the state machinery, including the government and armed forces. The other was the generation of 'community development' groups organizing at a grassroots level to tackle practical problems directly, campaign for people's rights, and through these to empower people. Another factor that encouraged the growth of these groups was the availability of funding from sources external to Namibia, which were unwilling to support such overtly political movements as SWAPO, and operated in a climate that looked favourably on small-scale community development programmes. In the early 1980s many such community organizations arose, some encompassing particular sectors of society, including women, students and young people, some based on issues such as housing, law and labour.

Women's groups, for example the YWCA and Namibia Women's Voice (NWV) are both products of this flourishing of groups, as is the women's desk at the CCN. Much longer-standing but no less subversive are the church-based groups such as the Mother's Union and the Lutheran women's groups. Right-wing groups have also followed this lead. The international perspective characterized by the Business and Professional Women's Federation and the participation of women in the 1985 Nairobi conference to mark the end of the UN decade for women are also of importance.[3]

The YWCA in Namibia began in 1985, on the instigation of visiting members of YWCA South Africa. Agnes Tjongarero, YWCA president in Namibia described its aims as:

> To develop the women in Namibia. Our problem is that most of our ladies are grassroots people. No formal education . . . without husbands, and having a tough time . . . Our aim is to develop women in this country. OK, it will take very long, but that's what we want to do.

To this end, the organization has four branches in the North and four in the South. The work takes the form of small projects: sewing, gardening, knitting, child-care, and schemes in which women are sent to South Africa or Zimbabwe to train as instructors or kindergarten teachers and so on. Agnes describes the setting-up of – in this example – a sewing project:

> We had several meetings with women. Then we asked them what are their needs, what do they want. That's how we found out that sewing is one of the things they want. Because one of their problems is that they've got school-kids. Now if you don't have enough funds to buy school uniform for five children, it can be very expensive, so most of the women felt . . . if they can make them it will be cheaper. And in some cases, they want to make an income-generating project . . . to make beautiful things and sell them and make money and help themselves.

Fundamental to the community development approach is the concept of self-determination – the people concerned deciding their own priorities. Strauss links this with the consciousness-raising aspect of development work:

> We begin to realize the necessity of the people's wealth of knowledge and no longer patronize them . . . Honesty in attacking problems so as to alleviate suffering is a precondition for success, especially in liberating the mind of the delusions created by apartheid.[4]

Tjongarero is clear that through a seemingly simple activity such as sewing, advances are made on the practical front in an increase in income; on the personal and social front, through self-confidence and skills learning; and on the political front both through the challenge to a system that subordinates women by denying them education, training and means of income, and through raising awareness.

> The reason for financial problems is lack of education, because if you don't have education, where are you going to get work from? I mean proper work with a proper salary . . . If you don't have work you don't have money. It's as simple as that. On the other hand, why are most of the women and even men uneducated? It's because of the government system. You know that in our black schools the level of education is low. If they can read and write it's enough you know. And it's not enough . . .
>
> Why are the women less educated? Cultural things . . . it's not necessary for a girl to be educated. Why? After all, she'll get married and someone else will look after her . . . So we usually say women are oppressed in many ways. It's not only the system which is oppressing them but also their husbands, their fathers and so on.
>
> Awareness of oppression is not a primary focus of the work, but is integral to it and occurs naturally. We talk about these oppressions. Projects are about becoming conscious, but we don't call that a project – it's just ordinary talk.

In the women's movement as much as in community development, it has long been a theme that women must determine their own priorities by giving recognition and value to their own experience. It is perhaps due to the recent emergence of these groups that this concept is adhered to. Their approach to development is therefore one of autonomy, seeking to empower women, rather than what can be termed a 'welfare' approach, in which women are beneficiaries in their role of mothers and home-makers, or an 'efficiency' approach, in which although it is recognized that programmes will not be effective without women's participation, women's real needs are secondary to those of the project. In addressing developmental issues, such organizatons as the YWCA and NWV are making a statement about the gender perspective of development; addressing the specific needs of women as autonomous producers, reproducers and managers within the community.

The needs, related to these roles, that women traditionally play, may, for the sake of clarity, be divided into two categories: 1) the purely practical, relating to their productive and reproductive roles (health care, childcare, food processing and marketing, for example), areas catering to the needs of the family and community. And 2) those that are strategic, addressing the needs of women as individuals, arising from their role as subordinate to men. Four areas which strategic needs might approach can be distinguished: alleviating domestic care and labour; providing women with their own independent income; abolishing the sexual division of labour; and removing discrimination in terms of rights to property or rights over their own bodies.

The YWCA is still relatively small in Namibia, but illustrates that women's strategic needs can be tackled through modest activities such as sewing or gardening. These activities could be perceived as traditional, inasmuch as they relate to the reproductive and productive roles of women, (sewing, however, is not a tradition in Namibia and for these women it is a new skill to be learned). But in fact they are radical on the level of race, class and gender, as they challenge and change the women's role as subordinates. This theme is echoed in all the 'progressive' women's groups, one of the most vocal being NWV, which has a more overtly feminist approach. Staff expressed its role as: 'Being a support to feminists who are often isolated. We are also active in giving confidence to women and helping them realize there is a problem'. This is done through practical projects at a grassroots level but also at times through national campaigning work.

> We are supporting the struggle through projects used for mobilization. We are part of the workers movement and engage in practical means of support, for instance through supporting the student uprising. [This interview was made at the time of the student boycott of 1988]

Like YWCA, NWV is a national organization, but at a local level, the groups determine their own priorities, and like YWCA the activities therefore tend to address the strategic and the practical needs simultaneously. Lindy Kazombaue, co-ordinator of NWV describes this process:

We give a framework to individual branches, but priorities for activities are left to them. Projects must be developmental, i.e., within a context of educating the women. Everything must be done with awareness training. The system is that the branch meets, and problems are expressed and priorities established.

In Windhoek for example, the priority was to create jobs, so we set up a needlework co-op, making African dresses. This has been successful, but it's difficult to compete with the chain stores, so we want to set up a shop for the products of the people, including traditional food. There is already a shop like this in the North. In the North, the high failure rate of schoolchildren is also a priority so there is a lot of organizing round this.

In the NWV branch at Keetmanshoop, in the South of the country, there is also a handicrafts project. The representatives there were clear on the objectives behind the work.

It is to help women's self-sufficiency, to teach new skills, to answer what the women asked for, and to raise their self-esteem through achievement. Most important is that women raise their consciousness and self-esteem. We are not ready for independence here in the South. There is a utopian view of independence, whereas the reality is that it will be hard. If a woman doesn't think well of herself, she can't help her children. Even if she can't read or write, she is still a mother and an educator and doctor and administrator, with so many skills she doesn't recognize because society doesn't recognize them.

We want to teach them that all women are the same. Here, on the street, black women shrink from white women. Our hope is that our children can grow up and know their rights. Our problem is inferiority complex imposed by the system. We can't be fully productive because we think we are less than we are.

The Keetmanshoop group also addresses other problems:

The main problems for us here are non-school attendance, early pregnancies, often in standard six at the age of thirteen, drug and alcohol abuse, housing, and income. Wages are on average R30-R40 a month. There is often no husband, and six children on a single income. All the money goes on rent. They are evicted when they can't pay, and they erect a shanty house in the backyard of a friend. They must pay also for this.

Since May,[5] we started an educational programme. We invited all the principals of local schools to discuss the problem of non-school attendance. To find a solution with mothers, fathers and teachers together. . . . The parents don't know the children don't go to school. They are out early at work and late back. The children don't get proper food or proper sleep – the houses are overcrowded and the fathers drink and keep them awake at night. Also violence in the family and early sex and pregnancy keeps them

> from school. And the children need to find jobs or crime to supplement their income.
>
> So we came up with two solutions. One is to provide food on the school grounds, and the other is for the parents to have better support to get the kids to school and go to the teachers.

It is indicative of the hard battle that faces this kind of endeavour, that at the time of the interview, no action had been taken, as only one school principal attended the meeting.

## Political implications

Namibia Women's Voice also works on a national level. Leadership training courses are run for women from the local groups, and a campaign against the use of Depo Provera has been an important national project, using both awareness-raising methods in the local groups, and campaigning work aimed at the government and the Upjohn company. A second campaign was directed at right-wing propaganda 'low-intensity warfare' groups, which adopt the community organization model in order to exert influence.

> The government's propaganda campaign to win the 'hearts and minds' of the people through groups like Etango and Ezuva[6] is pernicious, particularly in the rural areas. Voice is raising awareness of these groups. It is essential to develop people before these groups offer them money, and so on, and this is what we are trying to do.

NWV, like YWCA and other development groups, was conceived in the mid-1980s. An acknowledged contributory factor to this, as was outlined with regard to YWCA was the interest of foreign aid agencies in work with women, and the practice of many such agencies of not supporting overtly political work. Lindy Kazombaue describes the organization's inception:

> We started because there was no ecumenical women's group. In the early 1980s, some women were in a political group and church women were in separate non-political groups. There was no developmentally orientated group. At that time, visitors from overseas were asking to see women. Dr Shejavali [of the CCN] convened an informal group which acknowledged the need for a platform to talk about ordinary problems. There was a consultation in 1984, and in 1985 the first meeting was held in Windhoek.

Sadly, NWV's history has been dogged by uncertainty and non-co-operation with other groups and individuals. It is impossible and inappropriate for us to judge the rights and wrongs of such disagreements, but it is important to take note, if only as an example of the difficulties women's organizations can face. NWV's political position was perceived as ambiguous, its opponents claimed that it had been divisive, drawing people away from the SWC, failing to consult with the other progressive groups, that it was open to infiltration as there were insufficient checks on membership, and that the sources of its funding were unknown, and might not have been politically acceptable. (Progressive groups scrupulously check their sources of funding to guard against manipulation by right-wing organizations.)

On the question of funding, it is true that Namibia Women's Voice was fortunate in attracting money through their development projects, which met the criteria of funding organizations. This allowed them to grow very quickly. By 1986 there were already 13 branches, and they were equipped with a vehicle, an office and three full-time workers. This was obviously keenly felt by the barely funded SWC, which, as a political organization, could not meet the criteria of development funders, and YWCA, which has to go through Geneva for any financial help. NWV said they were willing to be open about their sources of funding but not prepared to submit to the direction of a political party. This reluctance may partly account for their alleged lack of consultation. For Kazombaue there are sound reasons for having an open membership:

> Politics is a segregator. Voice is open to all women who accept the constitution which is committed to resolution 435, and has a strict policy of not working with the system. Most of the women in Voice are church women, mainly apolitical . . . either because they are not conscious or because they are afraid, or because of the traditional role of women, politics being traditionally a male issue. Everyday struggle for survival is taking up women's energies. 435 doesn't refer to women's everyday realities. Voice's view is that we must work at both simultaneously. We are preparing for independence with women inside [Namibia]. . . We have to uplift people now in order that they can take part in the struggle.

Supporters of NWV claim that the opposition stems from NWV's success and from its challenge to male authority in both the churches and political parties. In the opinion of one staff member: 'There is a feeling that women's liberation is holding up the struggle, – that it's a distraction'.

At the time of writing this conflict was in abeyance due to the voluntary disbanding of NWV in March 1989, 'for the sake of maintaining peace and good relations' and in order to unify resources for preparation of the election.' This account of the conflict does, however, illustrate the problems of a liberation movement in the context of multiple oppression. Several of our interviewees were of the opinion that the conflict was fuelled by men, particularly in the churches and political parties, 'so that they can dismiss women as typically having problems', as one NWV staff member expressed it. Hilma Shilongo Pauli echoed this viewpoint: 'Women are still oppressed. In the eyes of men they are competing with each other'. One senior statesman upheld the view that men are resentful:

> In the African situation, the question of women is a theory issue even to some on the leadership. They pay lip-service to women's liberation so long

as it doesn't happen in the home.

The issue is hotly debated, and a wide spectrum of opinion expressed; at one extreme, women as well as men agree with one female member of staff at CCN, that 'our main struggle is against the Boers. The women's issue isn't really as important.' On the other hand, many women choose to be members of both NWV and SWAPO, maintaining the view that conflict between the organizations is unnecessary.

Despite the obvious resistance to the concept of dual oppression, it is clear that through trying to meet some of the strategic needs of women, women's organizations are challenging, not only the state, but the status quo among their own people. It is perhaps this issue that underlies some of the arguments for delaying development work until after independence. But as Agnes Tjongarero says, referring to development and politics, they need not be seen to be in conflict:

> It's the same thing. Maybe on different levels or so on, but it's the same thing. If you take the women's council of SWAPO, it's the same thing. They are also trying to develop the women.

The supposed conflict between development and resistance is rooted in an absence of gender perspective on either. As we have seen with the work of NWV and YWCA, women's development is both a force of resistance and leads to active resistance. Equally, however, as the SWC experience testifies, women's resistance in the national struggle can lead to their development at some level, the problem then being, as Dan Tjongarero pointed out that this progress is not recognized.

Through the activities of these groups, women are grappling in a practical way with the problems of class, gender and racial oppression, and how to confront them. Emma Mujoro expressed the immediacy of this task as she spoke of the three oppressions:

> We cannot sit back and then start working. We have to prepare people now. This makes me strong . . . Women are so oppressed, they come to adopt it as their way of thinking. It must be broken. I will support and contribute as a priority. We will stand up and be shaken.

## Right-wing reactions

Meanwhile, the government was jumping on the bandwagon and sponsoring women's organizations. One strategy was an attempt to subvert the YWCA in its initial stages – an attempt that failed, as Agnes relates:

> Some of the ladies on the executive were pro-government women, and some were radicals, and there was conflict between the two groups. Now the YWCA is a non-governmental organization. And the situation in Namibia is such that if you are a pro-government person you can't work with the masses. It's impossible. So then we had big trouble on the executive

> committee of the YWCA which led to some people being expelled from the committee.
>
> I am working at the hospital, which is a government institution so I was called in by my bosses and given a warning . . . They wanted me to write a letter to the Cabinet and to apologize but I said I was not going to do.
>
> Anyway we got rid of those ladies and got on with our job. The problem now was that before we got rid of those ladies, the government was very much in favour of the YWCA, and said they would give us money. After the expulsion, there we are with problems like not having enough money.

Another government strategy as we have noted, was to support right-wing organizations. One such, the Rigters (Guides) was established to encourage support for the government among women. The importance of women in building up the economy and maintaining the status quo was emphasized. A spokesman for the organization said: 'South West Africa/Namibia, as an emerging independent country, will need all the manpower she can muster', and went on to praise the successes of private enterprise and to stress that women were needed to develop a sound economic base in the country, particularly as they had a larger capacity for detailed work than men.

The approach is one of 'efficiency', recognizing the strategic importance of involving women in programmes for the future, and fostering the growth of a middle class who will be reluctant to challenge the status quo. Its economic theory was founded on the current system, that is, the availability of a large uneducated labour force. The organization is supported by the right-wing churches, notably the Dutch Reformed Church. Unlike the progressive groups that operate on the basis of self-determining of priorities, and encouraging awareness and analysis, the Rigters engaged in propaganda against the theology of liberation and against communism. This organization was dominated by whites, with some 'coloured' members, but had little capacity to involve black women.

Other groups were formed as part of the government's attempt to win the 'hearts and minds' of the Namibian people. The DTA also set up small community development projects such as sewing and gardening in the South, as part of the 'low-intensity war conflict', (see chapter one). As a counter body to the CCN, the Namibia Churches Council was established, targeting the right-wing; the South African Red Cross also operates on a 'welfare' provision level. These groups, directly or indirectly formed part of the government's 'low-intensity warfare', while both NWV and the Contextual Theology Unit of the CCN attempt to monitor and increase people's awareness.

## Church-based groups

Women's groups associated with the churches occupy positions across the whole political spectrum, from those associated with the white Dutch Reformed Church to those associated with the black churches in the North.

The Anglican Women's Fellowship's (AWF) position is somewhere in the middle of this spectrum. Its aim is to remain apolitical and concentrate strictly on religious matters (fellowship, service, prayer, bible study, mission and witness), and some socially orientated projects such as knitting jumpers for children and old people in Katutura community centre. Some projects are purely church-orientated such as making hassocks, and the organization of a national clergy wives gathering, supported by Rossing, every two years. This meeting is ostensibly: 'to give wives more idea of places husbands are travelling to, and give them more confidence and to teach them to be good priests' wives'.

Membership, however, comprises white, black and coloured women, meeting to share things in common, and in the Namibian context this is progressive. Feminism must be defined in relation to the appropriate cultural context, and in the Third World context of Namibia, the simple act of women meeting across race barriers is progressive.

One reason for AWF's capacity virtually to ignore the political situation is that its branches are located outside the northern war zone. The members of the Mothers Union, another organization with a tradition at least as conservative as the AWF, live mainly in the war-torn North and therefore cannot escape being affected and involved. In this situation, the MU took a strong stance in opposition to the South African occupation. Like the YWCA and NWV, these groups deal with women's immediate experience, but in a context of prayer. Joyce of the MU explains:

> The women in the Mothers Union are married, everyone with a child. They have a duty to do something for the community. To do this, they meet in groups. The women have a duty to pray. They also do bible study. At the end of the prayer, some are just crying. Everybody is in difficulties.

Just as the churches decided to take a stand against the state (see the following chapter), the process moves the groups to take action. Joyce gives an example relating to the schools boycott:

> Now we are writing a letter to the AG [Administrator General], protesting about the military bases and supporting the children who are boycotting. This has to be seen first by the Bishop, then we will send it.

The Mothers' Union also joined with the Lutheran women to march to the minster of Owambo to discuss the problem. In fact the MU's history in Namibia and its recent renewal have been rooted in radical action. Founded in the 1960s by Isabel Hudson, an Anglican development worker, it grew quiet on her expulsion from the country in 1973. Vistorina recounts:

> It started again when the war became bad, 1980–81 when our priests and archdeacons were in jail. The mothers started again; meeting in groups, praying for the priests and taking action, writing letters and so on. Most of them were released.

It is the nature of war as the MU recognizes, that it is impossible to separate politics from other spheres of life:

> We are not free. If we get up and talk, then people say we are talking politics and they are afraid. One of my assistant sisters was taken away last week. At Ondehaluka, our teachers were beaten up yesterday. The headmaster saw but left. Here no political meetings are allowed so only church groups meet. So we say these things through the church. We say it in Nama [one of Namibia's indigenous languages] so they don't understand we are talking politics.

The Mothers Union is large in the North. There are 16 branches in Namibia, mainly in Owambo, one of these, at Odibo, has more than 100 members. Apart from mutual support and direct action against the state, the MU also engages in welfare and 'service' work in the parishes, where they have an important role in visiting the sick, organizing funerals, helping refugees from Angola, and similar activities.

Education in practical and social skills in connection with women's reproductive and productive roles is offered, that is hygiene, food preparation and first aid, the effects of alcohol, 'how to behave as women in the home, church and community' and so on. The work has also led directly to challenging women's subordinate role.

> We women in Namibia want to be recognized as the men are. We do the work which the men also do. We do more . . . We want to stand up in Namibia so that they can see we have difficulties, because before, they have never seen us. Before, only the men have been seen and heard.

Elizabeth Namundjebo is also active in the Mothers' Union:

> What I want for the Mothers' Union is for it to educate the women that they have a right to say things and give points of view, especially in this colonized country. It is also for the Mothers' Union to look after a member who might be arrested, or follow up one who is killed. We must know we have the right to follow up family members who are arrested. I want women's rights.

The Mothers' Union illustrates the inextricable nature of development organization and resistance and the gender perspective on both. Here, where violent repression forces one to live in fear, women are empowered to take action and in so doing, change and challenge their traditional role.

The Lutheran women's organization is also based in the North, run from an office at Ongwediva by Wilhelmina Shikomba, one of the first women theology students at the Lutheran seminary in Otjimbingue. Like the Mothers' Union, the Lutherans were propelled into a radical position by the war, as seen in their protest in support of the schools boycott (see chapter 5). Again like the Mothers' Union, social action and developmental work arose out of a primarily religious group:

> When we started in 1974 the women were just interested in reading the Bible, but after some years, they decided that they needed something else. They need to learn hygiene, knitting and so on, and they also need childcare. And because of these difficulties in our country, they told me and those who are on the committee that they also need to learn psychology.

Practical skills are taught: first aid, sewing, cooking for times of drought, and self-sufficiency from the expensive commercial sector:

> People are losing their skills in these days and think they have to buy expensive cake flour to make bread. We say, because you don't have money, that doesn't mean that you are poor.

There are also Bible and English classes:

> Ordinary women are learning English, because they want to read the newspapers. They want to hear – maybe there is something said in connection with their children abroad.

Shikomba remembers that the Lutheran women did not start off with theories of participative learning and prioritizing, but had to discover them:

> We found out that the women have also to do something. They have to write, for instance, some news so that others can also read. That is why we have this magazine for women called Kahewa, Our Friend. It has articles . . . about the women who have to educate their children at home, a recipe of how to cook biscuits, one about women with alcohol problems . . . How to help the man to be at home with their families and so on.

In both the Mothers' Union and the Lutheran Women's groups, meeting together is an act of resistance. Active opposition to the regime nourishes and inspires self-empowerment through development education, and vice-versa.

Other church-based women's groups have differing levels of activity. The small Methodist church in Windhoek for example, follows a welfare provision model in the form of a regular soup kitchen. The Catholic church has women's projects under the auspices of its social services department, which also address women's need for self-sufficiency in income, with emphasis on self-help.

## International aspects

The Namibian Business and Professional Women's Federation (BPWF) is a branch of the international organization. This is also true for YWCA and some of the church groups, but BPWF has an internationalist focus. All members in

Namibia are white except one, Hilma Shilongo Pauli:

> But [she says] the whites are nationalist [pro-independence]. The organization has a right to approach governments, and it is a way of meeting women from other parts of the world. The Organization can say things with the authority of an international voice. That's why I stick with it.

This authority has been used by the group to challenge the administration in Owambo on matters concerning them. This was overt campaigning on issues of class, race and gender:

> In 1981, we had a conflict with Kalangula [head of the Owambo administration under the 'second-tier' system of apartheid local government]. BPWF has the right to approach the authority so we sent a memo protesting that it was only black children that were sent into the army under eighteen; that the salary of men and women should be equal, and that there should be maternity leave provisions. He enforced some things, equal pay for equal work, but not maternity leave. In 1984, we went again to Kalangula. If a girl is pregnant before marriage, traditionally the father must pay R400 or R600 maximum, or a cattle. Then the man is free. We said 'We don't want the man to pay once. He should support the child till it is eighteen years old'.

For these women the struggle is a political one, well aware of the conservative nature of aid as patronage.

> He [Kalangula] suggested we start a welfare organization. We talked to an advocate in Windhoek about the Maintenance Act in the South. We said to Kalangula the Act in the South was good; that we wouldn't start a welfare organization, and that sex education should be started in schools.

This organization's internationalist nature serves to show that the international context has been of profound importance for the development of all the progressive groups. By the end of the UN Decade for Women, a climate more favourable to the advocacy of women's rights and development began to prevail. As already noted, visitors to Namibia asked to speak to women, and funds became more readily available for women's initiatives. It is outside the scope of this book to examine the reasons for this more favourable climate, but it is encouraging that for most progressive groups mentioned here the 1985 Nairobi conference to end the UN Decade for Women was an influential factor.

For the YWCA: 'There was a group of ladies who went to Nairobi, formed the steering committee and after Nairobi the executive members of YWCA South Africa came here'. Similarly for NWV:

> In 1985, 20 women were sent to the UN Women's decade conference . . . the issues taken up afterwards were family planning – Depo Provera – abortion,

> abandoned children, social problems, including violence in the family and so on.

Representatives from the Mothers' Union and Lutheran women and BPWF also attended the Nairobi conference. It is therefore in an international context that the dialectic of the struggle against class gender and racial oppression occurs for women. This in itself has been an empowering and activating influence. It has also enabled Namibian women to learn from the experiences of women in other countries which have fought liberation struggles. For example, on the question of delaying the fight for women's rights until independence, Hilma has this to say:

> We know from other African countries. We work with the men now and educate the whole country. We work for independence and human rights now. It's no good talking about rights of blacks if at the same time women are being oppressed.

## Conclusion

In this chapter we have examined the rise of community development and the women's movement that has grown from working in these ways. We have attempted to bring out the subversive nature of women meeting together inasmuch as it implies mobilization of a subordinate group in society. In addition, we have seen how the activities of these groups in seeking to fulfil practical and strategic needs of women, engage in the dialogue of the relationship between class, gender and racial oppression, and that all three are tackled. This is the revolutionary nature of sewing classes. 'Progressive' therefore needs to be defined within the Namibian context. Some groups as we have seen, by actively supporting the regime are repressive rather than progressive. Others illustrate the ability of human beings to accommodate complexities and contradictions in what they are engaged in.

It remains finally to cast a glance at the future. 'Nairobi: Forward Looking Strategies' states:[7]

> As the primary objective of development is to bring about sustained improvement in the well-being of the individual and of society and to bestow benefits on all, development should be seen not only as a desirable goal in itself but also as an important means of furthering equality of the sexes and the maintenance of peace.

That sexual equality is an integral part of development has by no means gained a consensus of opinion in Namibia. We have seen in relation to the SWC, however, that it is clearly SWAPO's policy for an independent Namibia and that the experience of women in other liberated countries has made Namibian women deeply aware of the pitfalls. It will certainly be an advantage in the future that independent groups have advanced so far in their practice and theory, that the ground is already prepared for work at a grassroots level on a much larger scale. It may also be an advantage that international links have been forged; groups such as the YWCA and BPWF are able to exert pressure that smaller groups cannot, as was remarked by one Namibian leader in relation to YWCA, that it is much more difficult for politicians to oppose an organization with links to an international body.

Women will certainly continue to organize in the future and to press for the advancement of women, and doubtless the groups will continue to be as diverse and at times as contradictory as they have been. There is a tolerance and a clear prioritizing of the personal aspects of women's lives, reflected in the words of Hilma Shilongo Pauli as she spoke of the most important message she had brought back from Nairobi:

> I learnt that as women we have a difficult task. The few who understand the struggle just carry on. Wherever you see a thing done by a fellow woman, support it. It doesn't matter if it's not 100% right. The main thing is to support and not to put criticism in the foreground.

# 8. 'A voice for the voiceless'

## The churches

> The Spirit is telling me that if I become anunChristian person, it's like a soldier throwing away his gun. Where am I going to go if I don't want to be a Christian any more? What will I do?

Such was the response of Mrs Shanghala, an elderly resident of the North when asked to explain what her faith meant to her. Living in the war zone and constantly at risk and under stress, she felt that her Christianity was the key to her survival. Her statement testifies to the central importance of the church in Namibia.

Around 80% of Namibia's population is estimated to belong to its churches which, since the 1960s have played a crucial role in protesting against South African oppression and calling for independence. No other network exists that can communicate with and unite the people to the same extent, and no other body is able to speak on their behalf with equal authority. But the churches' conversion to resistance is a relatively new development; the early missionary church was an integral part of the German invasion and occupation.

### The establishment of the church in Namibia

Missionaries were already present in the territory at the time of the German annexation, in 1884. Lutherans from the Rhenish Mission (RMS) arrived in 1844, and Finnish Lutherans in 1870. The German Roman Catholics came slightly later, in 1894, and the Anglican and Dutch Reformed churches moved in after the South African takeover in 1915.[1]

Missionary involvement from the outset paved the way for colonial invasion. Keen to establish themselves in Namibia, the RMS called for annexation, and encouraged German businesses to expand into the territory. Mission-Handels-AG, a limited company founded in 1873, concentrated on importing weapons and ammunition into Namibia; half its profits went to the RMS.[2]

The churches' complicity in the German conquest is illustrated most forcefully by their attitude to the war of 1904–06, when the Germans, with the utmost brutality, put down the uprisings among the Herero and Nama peoples. Far from trying to prevent this, the missionaries had called for war as a means of ensuring the survival of the missions, which at this point were under threat. They did not protest against the notorious extermination order of the German general, von Trotha, under which all members of the rebel groups were to be put to death. Many of the clergy actively helped the German troops.[3]

Other missionary activities, if less spectacular, were perhaps more far-reaching in their establishment of white domination. The church here, as elsewhere outside Europe, took a negative view of the local people and their culture and strove to impose their own values; racist attitudes were the norm. Their economic activities played a part in disrupting traditional African society and they also came to depend on the system of migrant labour. In 1907, the Catholic church declared an internal ban on marriages between people of different races, even before the Mixed Marriages Act came into force. Churches profited from the 1904–06 war by acquiring land previously farmed by Hereros and Namas.[4]

Church leaders in Namibia today, who are the descendants of the people who suffered at the hands of the missionaries, are the first to condemn the church's history. Pastor Zephaniah Kameeta, deputy bishop of the Evangelical Lutheran Church (ELC):

> The colonizers came like a pack of wolves . . . The people with good news came, but they turned to oppression and the good news became bad news for the poor. The missionaries were an easy and compliant tool in the hands of the powerful. They preached in a way that supported the system, and gave no dignity to human beings. Injustice was explained to the people as the will of God and not to be taken seriously in comparison to what they would get after death. Miserable conditions were explained as God's will.
>
> They attempted to reconcile the oppressed with injustice. Our great-grandfathers refused, and took up arms, and more than 60% of them were exterminated. For the rest there were concentration camps and the forced labour system.
>
> The survival of the church in these circumstances is a miracle.

Kameeta stressed the compliant mentality that the missionaries aimed to cultivate in their subjects. An interview with an old-age pensioner in Tsumeb, who received her early religious education in the 1920s and 1930s, underlined this point. Having complained at the unfairness of the government, she said: 'I will accept that as it is. That is my lot, so I will accept it. I am satisfied in that'. Her translator, a pastor, added his own explanation:

> Religion plays a very important role, especially for our old people, so that when something happens, they just accept it – maybe it is the will of the Lord. They are not like us, the young people, who say no, we want to make a change, because God is not so unfair. But for them, their religion taught them early – the missionaries just educated them like that – that they must accept everything. It is the will of God and in the hands of God, and that is that. What she is saying is an example of maybe all Namibian old women.

The missionaries' conduct had few redeeming features. It has been argued, for instance, that they helped to blunt the sharp edge of white brutality to blacks by stressing that killing black people, having sex with them or encouraging them to drink were unacceptable forms of behaviour. But all this was done within a context of racism[5] and, in any case, the effectiveness of such statements was doubtful.

The most lasting and positive contribution of the early churches was the establishment of social services. Their schools, hospitals and other institutions were of great importance in the almost complete absence of any state provision for black Namibians.[6] But in this area, too, the missionaries profited from colonialism. Many of their conversions came in after the 1904–06 war, when the surviving Hereros and Namas were imprisoned in concentration centres. The missionaries made it their business to provide welfare services for them and to harvest their souls in the process.[7]

Many of the churches' social services, too, were run on racist lines. The Lutheran and Catholic churches, for instance, had separate hospitals for whites and blacks, and the Catholics spent a disproportionate amount on the education and health of whites, despite the fact that there was state provision for this group.[8]

## Women and the early churches

For women in particular the early experience of the missionaries' colonialism was harmful. Suffering the break-up of their traditional values and the introduction of an alien culture, Namibian women were forced to conform to a morality even more oppressive to them than to men. They were also, like their men, drafted into the new order as servants and subordinates.

Nashilongo Elago of Namibia Women's Voice, herself a Christian, gave her interpretation of the effects of the coming of Christianity on women.

> Colonialism meant the division of the family, rape by whites and the destruction of traditional culture. Church buildings were important, and women were used as servants. Christianity is still foreign. It did away with my being a human being. God is still seen as a white, male, rich God.
>
> The churches brought new policies. Excommunication was very humiliating, especially to women. People were forced to abandon their traditional drinks, and the traditional wedding custom of marrying without a husband was abolished, giving rise to stigma because of an illegitimate child.

The traditional wedding referred to is a process whereby a group of girls who have attained a certain age are married. For some there will be husbands, for others not. The ceremony confirms the group as adults and makes it more acceptable for them to have children. Mrs Shanghala, an Anglican born about 1928, was forced into a traditional wedding despite her conversion to

Christianity. She described the ceremony:

> My parents used to believe in all kinds of traditional things, all kinds of evils. A traditional marriage is quite close to what is happening in the church. We used to wear goat-skins, and we had to go and do traditional dancing, and there was a horse's tail that was waved around in the air.
>
> This kind of wedding is not done in the homestead. I was taken to Ombalantu, and for the whole week I had to do traditional dancing. The brides usually stay for about five days without eating or drinking, and the day before they leave for their homes, they are given water to drink. In this kind of traditional wedding you don't have a husband yet. You just get married like that, without a boyfriend.

Even though the coming of the missionaries was a disaster in many ways, some women found conversion a liberating experience. Mrs Shanghala described how she became a Christian:

> We used to get a visitor called Titus Chimbule, who came to our place, and taught some songs. One of the songs was saying, 'my sister or my brother, why are you not a Christian, why don't you want to wake up and work for Jesus?' So I thought about that a lot, and then I decided to leave also, to work for the missionaries.
>
> I was a big girl, but not too big, and I went away because, in those years, not everybody wanted to become a Christian. Sometimes the father was against the children changing.
>
> When I first went away to the missionaries, I worked for them, as a cleaner and so on. We used to stamp the corn, and cut the grass, and keep the missionaries' place clean.
>
> My parents were not happy about me becoming a Christian, and they caught me, took me away from the missionaries and put me in a traditional wedding. But there was no man for me then. Later I just went away and worked in a hospital, in a dispensary. I became a Christian again. I worked there for two years, and in the third year I met my husband, and we got married.

Mrs Shanghala's experience confirms Nashilongo's statement that women were used as servants by the missionaries. But from it also emerges a more positive view of the early church. For Mrs Shanghala, fleeing to the mission and breaking with traditional life seems to have been a way of finding freedom. Other questions arise from her story: what were the emotional consequences to her, and others like her, in abandoning the old beliefs and her own family? What effect did the coming of Christianity have on family structures?

Many more accounts need to be heard before such questions can be answered. In the meantime, it should be noted that, although the church depended to a large degree on colonial activity and incentives such as education for the extension of its power, it did not operate only through compulsion and it did open new horizons and spiritual experience to some of its members.

## The conversion of the church

The profound changes in the Namibian churches since their colonial beginnings are as a result of pressure from Namibians, who have forced the churches to respond to their concerns and to allow them a meaningful leadership role. The church today still retains many features of its missionary origins, but essentially it is a church composed of and led by oppressed Namibians, and speaks as such.

The first signs of change came after the end of the Second World War when an Anglican priest, Michael Scott, took the Nambians' case to the United Nations (at the cost of ostracism from his church).[9] At about the same time over one-third of the members of the RMS in the South, enraged particularly at the fact that the mission did not allow black pastors, left to form the black-led African Methodist Episcopal Church (AMEC). Their secession was followed in 1966 by the formation of a 'Church of the Community' (Oruuano), by Herero people who were also dissatisfied with the RMS. 'We knew that our church belonged to the people', they said. 'That gave us heart . . . This church has not been imported from Europe, it has arisen on African soil'.[10]

Although both churches later suffered something of a decline (partly due to the fact that their ethnically-based position was in contradiction to the emerging consciousness of Namibia as one nation)[11] they were instrumental in pressing the Lutheran churches to grant independence to their branches in Namibia. In 1956 the Finnish Missionary Society, working in the North, became ELOC (Evangelican Lutheran Ovambo-Kavango Church). In 1960 it appointed Leonard Auala as its first black bishop. Meanwhile the Rhenish Mission Society was following a similar path, achieving full independence as the Evangelical Lutheran Church (ELC) in 1967. When, in 1963, the two churches amalgamated their theological training at the Paulinum seminary in Otjimbingwe, it was not only a sign of response to black demands, but also of a new spirit of co-operation and hope for unity within the Namibian nation.[12]

Similar movements within the other churches, prepared the way for their hierarchies to protest against certain political developments. For example, responding to the report of the Odendaal Commission[13] the Lutheran churches in 1967 prepared a memorandum objecting to the government's proposals. They later joined with the Anglicans in protesting against the treatment of prisoners in Owambo, but the process was slow. Although the Anglican bishop Robert Mize was expelled in 1968,[14] it was not until 1971 and the now-famous Open Letter that a position of open confrontation with the authorities was reached.

When the International Court of Justice decided in the same year that South Africa's rule in Namibia was illegal, Auala and Gowaseb, leaders respectively of ELOC and the ELC, were driven to write to the South African prime minister, Vorster. Taking as their starting point that 'South Africa, in its attempts to develop South West Africa, has failed to take cognisance of human rights, as declared by the UNO in the year 1948 with respect to the non-white population', they went on to comment:

> The non-white population is continuously being slighted and intimidated in their daily lives. Our people are not free and by the way they are treated they do not feel safe . . . 2. By the Group Areas Legislation the people are denied the right of free movement and accommodation within the borders of the country . . . 3. People are not free to express or publish their thoughts or opinions openly. Many experience humiliating espionage and intimidation . . . 4. We believe that it is important . . . that the use of voting rights should be allowed to the non-white population . . . 5. Through the application of Job Reservation the right to a free choice of profession is hindered and this causes low remuneration and unemployment. There can be no doubt that the contract system breaks up a healthy life because the prohibition of a person living where he works hinders the cohabitation of families.[15]

Couched in mild language and referenced throughout to the Universal Declaration of Human Rights, the Open Letter was nevertheless an indication of the shift within the churches and of the stand they were to take in the coming years.

The churches' resistance has involved them in supporting Resolution 435 and calling for sanctions against South Africa, as well as countless interventions on behalf of the Namibian people, and against human rights violations. In 1987, for instance, Bishops Kauluma, Dumeni and Haushiku brought an (unsuccessful) court action to have the curfew in the North lifted.[16] The resistance has also meant persecution, which has affected all except the right-wing churches. Attacks on the church became serious in the 1970s, particularly in the war zone, where demolition of church buildings and beatings of pastors and people became a common occurrence.

From about the same time, the Anglican church was consistently refused permits for its members to visit the North, and many of its workers, including three of its bishops, were expelled. The Anglican clinic at Odibo, near the Angolan border, had to be closed in 1974 because of suspected attacks committed by South African forces. The ELOC press at Oniipa, also in the war zone, was first bombed in 1973 shortly after the Lutheran leaders had led a delegation to Vorster (the press has subsequently been bombed twice, and resurrected each time). Lutheran and Catholic hospitals have come under threat, and some have been taken over by the government. The churches were also the target of disinformation campaigns that focus on accusations of communism, meddling in politics and alliance with SWAPO. Their answer is succcint: 'Whoever wants to teach us about communism, we want to teach about apartheid'.[17]

Hilma Shilongo Pauli, director of Christian Education of the Lutheran church in the North, confirmed that the message of struggle was supported throughout the church.

> At the grassroots level, the problem [of oppression] is accelerating. The sermons are changing. Even the congregations agree now. We don't just sit and be beaten and pray to be saved.

The importance of unity among the churches in order to campaign for independence has long been recognized. A powerful symbol of this recognition was the signing of the /Ai-//Gams[18] Declaration in April 1986. With the encouragement of CCN, most of Namibia's churches, some of its political parties (including SWAPO) and other organizations put their names to a document rejecting the South African occupation and the transitional government, calling for the implementation of Resolution 435, affirming 'our commitment to *One Namibia One Nation*, and promising related action.[19] The Declaration was followed by a Corpus Christi procession in June, which proclaimed the unity of the churches and their opposition to apartheid. This has become an annual event which, after 1986, was banned from going from Katutura into white Windhoek because, as one speaker at the June 1988 procession suggested, 'in a country which the South Africans have taken so much care to divide, unity is a very dangerous concept'.

The /Ai-//Gams declaration had been preceded in 1978 by the formation of the Council of Churches in Namibia (CCN), probably the biggest practical step towards the encouragement of unity.[20] (The CCN was in fact preceded by an ecumenical body called the Christian Centre.) All Namibia's major churches are members (with the exception of the white churches) and today the CCN, as well as running a wide range of social service programmes, is able to respond quickly and forcefully to events arising from the war and the South African occupation. Its role has been crucial during the transition to independence. As the UN High Commission for Refugee's partner, it has been responsible for receiving the 40,000 returning exiles, and it has also played an important part in monitoring the implementation of Resolution 435: CCN representatives obtained the first eye-witness accounts of the fighting that began on 1 April, something the corps of Western journalists present in the country was unwilling or unable to achieve.

The CCN's involvement in the repatriation of the exiles has been made possible by the work of women on the local and national levels. These women have had the task of welcoming the returnees into their homes. This function has been taken on with overwhelming enthusiasm by the women, who, often for the first time in more than ten years, have been meeting their children and relatives. Nangula Kathindi described how the CCN Women's Desk had held a week-long conference at which these issues were discussed:

> One of the very important topics was the return of our people from exile, and what is expected from us. And we were also grappling with the question of the implementation of 435, because at that time it was only two weeks after 435 had failed to be implemented – it was supposed to be implemented on November 1st [1988]. And the women were so disappointed. We are told that some people even developed high blood pressure from facing the fact

> that their children were not coming back, and they were not even sure whether it was going ever to be implemented.[21]

The churches' change of heart has been brought about and supported by changes in their leadership, their theology and the training of their workers. Wilhelmina Shikomba, who studied at the Lutheran seminary at Otjimbingwe in the late 1960s, compared what she was taught with a later syllabus.

> I can say that the theology taught there was Western. I think that it should be relevant to the people, to the blacks. That time I was there, I couldn't think very well about this, but when I started working, I thought that maybe it could be taught differently. Now there is a change, not like in our time.

The churches' theology has been transformed by the general acceptance of a Namibian version of liberation theology. This approach has been movingly stated many times; perhaps the best way to summarize is to quote Dr Shejavali, General Secretary of CCN, and Hilma Shilongo Pauli.

> The Church has no alternative but to proclaim judgement to the sinful situation . . . The Church is to take up Matt. 25:31-42 very seriously. We have many people in this country who do not have homes to stay in, food to eat, water to drink and clothes to wear . . . In our country there are many who have been brutally beaten up for no reason, who are in detention without trial and who are being tortured in the most cruel way . . . and it is all legalized action. For these, it is the task of the Church to bring hope to the hopeless and helpless people . . . the Church should make it top priority to comfort and console those who cry and mourn, to mobilize and conscientize people to expose the situation of oppression and be liberators of themselves . . . therefore, the masses should be taught to support all peaceful means aimed at eliminating apartheid – for instance, sanctions against South Africa should receive a strong supportive call from the Namibian Churches. We as CCN should be a movement striving for peace and justice that the name of God may be glorified in the land.[22]

For Hilma, the message was also one of practical reconciliation.

> Even in this situation [the war], we must pity misbehaving people. They are in the same house, the same family, the same nation. Joint action must be obtained to speak out about the war.
>
> Christian action is to tell those oppressors not to do so because it is against God's will, and to encourage those who are oppressed to say the truth and not to lose faith.

## Namibia's churches today: black and white

Before examining the position and role of women within the churches, it will be useful to summarize the structure of the present-day church in Namibia, and to consider the main cause of disunity within it: the profound division between black and white.

The Lutheran churches are the largest, followed by the Catholics. The ELC, led by Praeses Frederik, covers the South of the country, while ELCIN (the Evangelical Lutheran Church in Namibia, formerly ELOC) serves the North and has its headquarters in Oniipa, where its bishop, Kleopas Dumeni, is based. The Catholic church in Namibia is similarly divided into two geographical areas. The leadership of the southern diocese has a reputation for inactivity but, by contrast, the bishop of the northern diocese, Bonifatius Haushiku, is one of the leaders most ready to speak out against oppression. He is also one of the handful of black clergy in a diocese where foreign missionaries of the old school are still much more in evidence than in the other churches. This is not the case with either the Lutheran or Anglican churches, which have a high proportion of black clergy. The Anglican leader, Bishop James Kauluma, is also very outspoken; many of his church's members lived inside the war zone (because the early Anglican missionaries concentrated on the North). All the churches are members of CCN, as are the smaller Methodist, Congregational and AME churches.

The main churches on the other side of the racial divide are the Afrikaans-speaking Dutch Reformed Church (DRC), and DELK, the German Lutheran church. There are also other minor Afrikaner churches, and although the DRC only allows whites through its doors, it has 'mission churches' among other groups, particularly in the 'coloured' community. The Anglican and Catholic churches, despite their progressive leadership, also have conservative white minorities and are effectively segregated on racial lines because parish boundaries are based on residential areas. Where the Anglican church has made efforts to unify the churches of one town, particularly in Walvis Bay and Windhoek, it has met with stiff resistance from the white congregations.

Blatant racial discrimination is still the norm within the DRC. A woman in Keetmanshoop, for instance, reported the story of a 'coloured' woman who was not permitted to enter the DRC building for her white husband's funeral, solely on account of her skin colour. In Tsumeb, too, black residents expressed anger at the fact that graves of black people in the white town had been removed to make way for a new Dutch Reformed Church building. The bones had been surreptitiously reburied in the township graveyard, and, since this was now full, the people had been offered the site of a rubbish tip for their new cemetery. 'They think black bones are just rubbish', said one woman.

The causes of the white churches' racism are not hard to find. They reflect the gulf in society between most whites and most blacks. Only a few whites in the church are in agreement with the black majority. Benefiting from the system, white Christians have refused to accept that apartheid is unjust or to condemn the South African occupation, calling instead for a superficial reconciliation between conflicting groups in society.[23]

Zephaniah Kameeta summed up the role of the white churches:

> The past is still very much with us. The South Africans are carrying on from the Germans, and their god is a god of national security and law and order. He is a racist god. I don't accept that I am being persecuted by people who believe in the same god as us. He must be a different god.
>
> The evil and paralysing past is present in the hearts and minds of many people in Namibia. It is present in churches and sects and supported by the South African government and its surrogates. Their gospel is limited to the soul and heart, and for them the biggest sins are smoking, drinking, dancing and sex.

There have been some signs of movement within the white churches, even if it is on an individual basis. In Oranjemund, where many of the residents take pride in the integration of the mixed race schools and residential areas of the town, two white women described how they had moved from racist Afrikaner churches to become Anglicans. Both were still very distant from a black perspective, but both also now felt that they were distant from the churches of their parents, and under some social pressure. 'People come up to me in the street,' said one, 'and ask how I can belong to Tutu's church.'

## Women in the churches

Women have many places in Namibia's churches. They are workers and servants, they are nuns and a few are leaders. They gain and give spiritual and emotional support through worship and they do many of the practical, unrecognized tasks necessary to keep the church running. Most of all, they form the backbone of the congregations, particularly in areas where many of the men are away on contract or until recently were in exile. These women's commitment to the church was expressed by villagers in the Kavango who were attending literacy classes. 'If we know how to read and write', they said, 'we can read the Bible, and encourage ourselves in the Bible'.[24]

### Leaders within the church

All of Namibia's main churches recognize, in some way, the importance of women to them, but this recognition is often limited to the incorporation of a women's society within the church structure. These groups are often a means of diverting women's energy and demands rather than allowing them an authoritative role in the church hierarchy. 'It's clear that women are in a majority in the churches', said Nangula Kathindi, the CCN Women's Desk worker. 'They're participating more, but only in basic things, not of course in the full-scale work of the church, as pastors, priests or workers necessarily. Some teach only Sunday school, and that's not good enough'.

There are, however, some women leaders, particularly in the Lutheran church. Miss Gowases, an old-age pensioner, was elected an elder of the Lutheran church in Tsumeb after a lifetime of devotion to church work.

> When they elected me as an elder, five years ago, I decided to take on this career, because I was old enough, and I had no husband and I wanted to keep myself busy. So I thought this might be the right way.
>
> When I am sitting in the church service, and children are busy making noises, I am free to stand up and silence them because I see this as my duty. Also I translate from one language to another, and I light the candles on the altar, and put them out. For me, the altar is very holy.
>
> I have been in the church service for 45 years now, and I am active together with the other women in the church's work. At first I was giving Bible studies and so on.

From Miss Gowases, we gain a glimpse of the many leadership roles that women exercise in the church. To find women performing this kind of function is not uncommon. There are stories, for instance, of women who give religious instruction to the isolated families living on white-owned farms. When Ida !Ha-eiros was in gaol, she taught the Bible to her fellow prisoners. The church's recognition of these roles, however, is somewhat slow to catch up with reality. Women are permitted to be pastors within the southern Lutheran church (although not in ELCIN), but there are, as yet, very few of them and consequently their struggle for acceptance is hard. The Anglican church does not ordain women, neither of course, do the Catholics but there is movement among the Anglicans. The diocese of Namibia has voted to ordain women, but is not taking action until the church of the province of Southern Africa itself agrees to the measure. This is coming nearer: in June 1989 its synod voted by 121 to 79 to ordain women, but this fell short of the required two-thirds majority.[25]

For women like Miss Gowases, active Christianity and involvement in the church are the main motives for adopting prominent roles, which are often carried out primarily as a duty. But church leaders of a younger generation, to whom, like their elders, Christian spirituality is central, are also motivated by a consciousness of the secondary place of women in society and the church, and a desire to fight. One such is Rev. Emma Mujoro, a pastor at the Lutheran seminary at Otjimbingwe, who explicitly puts her approach to theology and the church in the context of women's oppression.

> Namibian women suffer three oppressions: white men, white women and black men.
>
> I can't stop or go back. I can't divide or cut my ideology from my theology. Women are also in the image of God. I have the same responsibility as men. I don't believe in an unrighteous God.
>
> There is one thing that is hurting me: that is that women are used as sex objects. Men can give us as many children as they like. Many are single women. Here at Otjimbingwe, some have thirteen children.

She described how she was trying to encourage a new approach through women's theology.

> It's a new perspective, especially here. We are approaching it through Bible studies. We use portraits of women we read about in the Bible, and ask, where can we find our way as women in the churches? For instance, Deborah was a mother, a judge, a prophet and a leader. God also uses women to spread the gospel.

Hilma also fulfils a leadership role in her job as ELCIN's director of Christian education:

> My office is to supervise the syllabuses which are taught, to ensure that they are up to standard and according to Christian teaching, and to ensure that training is done properly. We offer training on how to reach the people and help them, and how to explain Biblical texts and put them in the context of people's lives.

She had, however, experienced problems in doing her job. 'As a woman director working with men, it is difficult. I am not taken seriously. Even women don't take me seriously'.

The leadership of women like Hilma and Emma demonstrates a limited movement within the church towards recognition for women. A necessary preliminary for this has been the provision of theological training for them. This is not yet widespread: there is, for instance, a new Anglican seminary in Kombat which prepares for ordination men who already have practical experience of church work. The students are, of course, all men. But women were first accepted at the Lutheran seminary in Otjimbingwe in the late 1960s. Hilma, and Wilhelmina Shikomba, now the Lutheran women's officer at Ongwediva, were the first female students there. Wilhelmina remembered how she went there:

> After I reached standard 6, I did a training course, and then went to teach. After that I went to Otjimbingwe theological college. That time, it was only men who were taught there at Otjimbingwe, but one of the old pastors told me that they wanted women also to be taught theology. They convinced me that I could also go there. We were two at that time – the other person was Hilma.
>
> The subjects taught were hymnology, Biblical study, ethics, Christian ethics, dogma and Greek. I was there for four years, and I reached the ordinary qualification. That time, the year when some continue with the diploma, I felt that maybe I had to work, and I couldn't continue. But I also studied through correspondence and got my matric.

Women continue to be trained at the Otjimbingwe college, although they are still in a small minority. According to Wilhelmina, six had completed their studies there by 1988. Hilma also criticized the seminary for providing better opportunities to male than to female students.

**Women as servants**

Despite the tremendous changes in the church over the last 30 years, there are still ways in which CCN member churches are not yet liberated, and continue to oppress the people or to serve them inappropriately. Forms of worship, for instance, are still very much based on Western models, even though the vernacular is often used and an African element introduced through music. Women are the group most exploited by the modern church.

As well as their lack of recognition in leadership roles, women suffer the weight of church authority mainly in two ways: social pressure, and the use of their unpaid or underpaid labour.

We have already noted Nashilongo Elago's comments of how the coming of Christianity created a stigma against a woman with a child born out of wedlock. While it is debatable how far African people have really adopted the 'moral standards' of the West in this regard, it is certainly true that some of the churches, particularly the Anglican, are keen to enforce these standards. A (male) priest in the far north described how church discipline was exercised.

> People of all ages come to repentance classes, to revise their belief and the promises they made. The sins are adultery etc. There is some stealing. The people come voluntarily. The person confesses, they are given a Bible passage, especially the ten commandments. They learn them and revise the promises they made at baptism and confirmation.

The priest evidently felt that the classes were a constructive exercise in bringing people back to their faith. His statement that the people came voluntarily should, however, be seen in the light of the fact that the children of women who had 'sinned' by giving birth outside wedlock, were denied baptism unless their mother publicly repented.

The synod of the Anglican church has also voted to deny communion to unmarried couples who were living together. According to some proponents, this measure would mean greater protection for women, and had resulted in the prompt marriage of many such couples; but the Catholics have not issued such an edict. In Keetmanshoop one woman explained that it was normal for stable couples with several children to remain unmarried. To her, this situation protected women, as without a legal contract they still had the ultimate option of leaving, and she felt that this factor kept the men in order to some extent. She believed that any attempt by the church to change this situation would fail.

The church's use of women's labour parallels to some extent the use of this commodity by society as a whole. In the church as in general, husbands benefit from their wives' work. We have seen how the missions came to depend on women for domestic and farming tasks, and this is still largely true of the church as a whole. Priests and church workers of all denominations depend on women for the maintenance of their houses, care of their children, and the cleaning of church buildings and missions is usually left to them.

This dependence within the Anglican church is illustrated by the activities of the Anglican Women's Fellowship, which holds a clergy wives' gathering every two years. Intended to support the wives, who often have had a more restricted career than their husbands, these meetings also have the purpose of making the women into effective helpers for their husbands. For example on one occasion, the wives were taught how to wash and fold the altar cloth.

On Catholic missions, too, the priests depend on women's labour while the nuns do their own domestic work (sometimes with outside help). In 1988, this was the case at two such centres, one in the Caprivi and one in Owambo where, in addition, the men had adequate finances, while the women struggled and worked hard for little reward. In one case, women were responsible for running an institution with very few staff and therefore had to cope with a very heavy work-load. In the other, four nuns had to survive on the modest salary paid to one of their number, who taught in a church school; the other three helped to run the school, but were not paid for it. Such conditions do not apply to all the Catholic missions, but in all of them the inequality between genders is further emphasized by the contrast between women's status as nuns and men's as priests.

The story of Sister Josephine, of the Catholic mission at Keetmanshoop, illustrates the links between the church and women's domestic labour, but also adds another dimension to the story: 'From Standard 8, I went to domestic school. This is to teach us to be domestic workers, to make food, clean and so on'. The school was run by nuns, and while there Josephine had evidently been encouraged to join the order. When she eventually did so, it was a liberation from the sufferings of her childhood, when she had been regularly beaten and mistreated by relatives and her mother's lovers.

> I liked the school because of the feeling of love the sisters had for me. I said to myself that I must become something in my life, and I tried to do my best to become something in my life. I didn't have the desire to marry, and I also saw how many women didn't have a good life in their houses.

Any oppression from the church went unnoticed in comparison to the situation from which she had escaped.

**Protest**

It is difficult to generalize about how far Namibian women feel resentful of their treatment by the church hierarchy. For many, serving the church is an unquestioned way of serving God and of establishing a place within the community. But many also recognize the restrictions of their position and are seeking to change it. 'If the church is a voice for the voiceless, then let it be so', said Nashilongo Elago at the 1988 CCN conference. While remaining within the church, she is keen to reclaim it for women and was outspoken in condemning its oppression of them.

> The church concentrates on individual sin and ignores the primary causes of single motherhood, and the woman gets punished more.
>
> In church, the Bible is the liberator, but women are denied the right to fight with it through policies against the ordination of women, for instance. The church must open up. The Bible has been used to oppress us, but it can also be used to liberate us. In African independent churches women are bishops.

For Nashilongo, as for other leaders of Namibia Women's Voice, many of women's problems derive from the fact that the Namibian church was founded by Europeans. One of them explained that the struggle of Namibian women was similar to that of women in the West because:

> Church structures are the same in the West as here. A revision of the church is necessary. The women's struggle is everywhere, and cultural differences are not very important. The church has not been part of the struggle, and we want to make it so.
>
> The men don't want to hear. This is causing restlessness. God is a righteous God, and therefore cares about women's oppression.

So for these women, the struggle within the church is not simply about gaining recognition for women, but also about liberating the church to enable it to engage completely in the fight against apartheid. 'Liberation will allow women to participate in the struggle', said one. 'At the moment, the church is not ensuring that all its members can participate'. Nangula Kathindi also considered that women were being ignored, and related their struggle to the difficulties of young people within the church.

> It's older men still, and older people, who are dominating everything. They are also not listening. Young people feel that their ideas are not taken seriously. So the position of women in the church is really under question. Some doors have to be opened still for women, knowing that they are also human beings like men.'

She pointed out the need for consciousness-raising among women.

> I don't think the atmosphere should be coloured still by the feeling that 'I'm a woman, therefore I can't do this'. I think that we should really take seriously that we are all Christians, and we are all God's children, and we shouldn't make people feel different because you are a woman.

**Spirituality and struggle**

Most Namibians are Christians. Namibia is a religious society; the contrast with the secular West could not be greater. People expressed themselves through religious language and imagery, and asked for the message 'pray for us' to be taken overseas. The churches are the most important institutions in the country, and bishops and pastors are seen, along with the SWAPO leadership, as the true representatives of the people.

One factor encouraging the deep spirituality commonly found in the country has been the hard conditions the people faced, particularly in relation to the war. Women have found in their faith a way of surviving from day to day. The church has also been important in holding the communities together, particularly in areas where the curfew seriously restricted social life for the 15 years to 1989. The Sunday service is a big occasion, people may walk for several hours to reach the church, where they will spend two to three hours worshipping and listening to the choirs, composed of members of the congregation, which perform after the service.

Joyce, of the Mothers' Union in Ohangwena, then inside the war zone, explained how the local women were supported by praying together.

> One day in the week is chosen for prayer, when all are given the chance to pray for everything: the war, the schools boycott, the problem of imposters. Even when you are sleeping you are just afraid. You don't know if someone is coming to kill you or what.

Women working in the more liberated conditions of the independent schools, but constantly at risk from government repression, also expressed themselves in religious terms. Women teachers at Koichas school in the South asked people overseas 'to pray for our school, to pray for us the teachers, that we can continue with our work, and to help us where they can'.

In many societies it would be easy for this dependence on religious faith to become an escape route to the hereafter rather than an opportunity to awaken people to the need to change the present. But in Namibia, where the close links between the church and politics are recognized and the majority church took a bold stand in favour of liberation, this is not generally so. Many women were equally deeply committed to Christianity and to the struggle, which they see as inseparable. They protested against their situation, and went on to express their trust in God and their hopes of an end to the war and the South African occupation.

This outlook was illustrated by the black women of Oranjemund, most of whom were active in SWAPO, the union and the church. SWAPO Women's Council meetings alternated with church meetings, which were used for mutual support and encouragement. A member of the group explained that, 'women meet in SWAPO and in an ecumenical church group. There is a Bible study or a SWAPO meeting on Saturdays. Most of the black women go – they are quite highly politicized.'

> The church group operates as a support group where women talk about their problems. These include bringing up children, and housing problems. It is difficult to teach a child to follow our own culture when there is competition from school. We are working at preserving our own culture and giving children stability. All the women understand the importance of this.

Perhaps the experience of these women gives a clue as to why many failed to name oppression by the church as a grievance. In a world constantly subject to change, the church has offered them some security. For women in Oranjemund this has meant enabling them to pass on their culture to their children. In the war zone, the church provided a meeting place and opportunity for mutual support, as well as a voice to express the people's grievances. In all these situations women saw the South African occupation as the main cause of oppression and difficulties. That the church was fighting this, and therefore taking on women's most pressing demands, relegated its structural imperfections to second place.

One way of understanding Namibian women's outlook on their situation and their faith is to look at the Bible passages they chose as the most meaningful. Mrs Shanghala chose Psalm 22: 'My God, my God, why have you forsaken me? . . .', a choice that powerfully expressed how she felt about her situation, and how relevant was Biblical language to her despair.

Teachers at Koichas school also chose a psalm. Psalm 56 seems to balance the experience of persecution against a deep trust in God and faith in the power of resistance. 'Be merciful to me, O God, because I am under attack. My enemies persecute me all the time . . . When I am afraid, O Lord Almighty, I put my trust in you . . . What can a mere human being do to me?'

The more optimistic view of these women was also shared by Wilhelmina, who chose Revelation 21: 'Then I saw a new heaven and new earth . . .' 'The words of God that give me hope in this struggle', she said, 'is the promise that He will make a new heaven and a new earth where justice will be. And in that time, when justice and peace will rule among people, I think that is the time when we'll have peace among ourselves'.

## The future: Developing the women's struggle in the church

As we have seen, there are many signs that women within the churches are becoming increasingly vocal. One catalyst for change will be the CCN Women's Desk, part of its Contextual Theology Unit. Nangula Kathindi described the Desk's plans to mark the 'churches in solidarity with women' ecumenical decade of the World Council of Churches.

> We have proposed establishing local and regional ecumenical decade committees . . . We feel that people need to be aware about the developments in the country . . . people on the grass-roots level. We feel because Namibia is independent, true reconciliation has to be embarked on.
>
> We have also proposed contextual Bible studies. We will look at the examples of women in the Bible, and at reading the Bible through our own eyes, through the eyes of single parenthood . . . We can tackle the issue of single parenthood, widowhood because of the war, and also we don't want to overlook the issue of prostitution, and then domestic workers' situation and so on, and other ways women are oppressed.

> . . . we feel that women theologians must come together and speak out on their own situation in the church. There are women who have indicated that they want to be ordained, but they are not given a chance. We will also try to publish what they have discussed.
>
> [Also there are] what we are calling Justice, Peace and the Integrity of Creation seminars. We would like to put a challenge to society from women, as far as these issues are concerned, and we thought we should invite women who have just come back from abroad and women who have been inside the country all along to these seminars. Women will come to learn about one another, share ideas, and tackle women's issues.

So the future for women in the church is seen as being closely connected with developments in the country, developments which themselves are to provide an opportunity for change that will benefit women. In particular, women are taking up the theme of reconciliation after the war. Sister Josephine summed this up:

> I want apartheid here to stop, and I want us to become one, to love one another and work together and help one another as brothers and sisters and children of God.

# 9. 'The only hope one has'

## Conclusion

Women all over Namibia are turning their thoughts to the future. There will without doubt be changes in women's lives, but the direction of these changes is still uncertain. The differences in Namibian life and politics between 1989 and 1988 were certainly startling. In June 1988 the negotiations between South Africa, Angola and Cuba were underway, but very few people inside the country believed that they would be effective. By August 1989, Resolution 435 was in progress, many of the refugees had returned home, and free and fair elections were a real possibility.

Two CCN staff members, Rosalind Namises and Nangula Kathindi, spoke about their hopes for the future. Nangula, looking forward to the gains that independence might bring for women said:

> I'm hopeful because many women who are educated have come back home. They have experience, not only of the West, but also in Africa, which is closer to our situation. One would hope that we women would come together and pull together, and make our voice heard, not only for the sake of speaking out, but also for the sake of bringing about change. Because the implementation of 435 is bringing change to the whole of Namibia, and women shouldn't be left out.

> I hope SWAPO wins the election [said Rosalind] and that we at last have a chance to go into many things, because that has been why I was involved. I was angry, I was desperate for a new government, and I hope that when SWAPO take over they will get us our goals we have been planning for. I hope there will be development for people – people will be educated, I think, and they need to be able to start doing things and start to take control of their own lives. And I hope that SWAPO, if it takes over, will be a very understanding government, and very warm when we come to complain or ask for some things, to give the community a chance to talk from the ground.

Like many other community leaders, she foresaw the dangers ahead. She had been assessing the effects of South African propaganda and destabilization in Namibia:

> I want to tell the communities that they must not think it's going to stop here. It will go on after independence because that's where the destabilization process will come in. The religious part [right-wing religion] will be used to fulfil that.
>
> Of course, I know that South Africa will never leave us alone, they will still be involved to destabilize us. But I think we have never tasted anything else beside South Africa, and for that reason also we will fight again so that what we want will come about. Because one can never be satisfied if you fight for something and you don't get it after some very important thing has happened, like elections. If we don't even get the people's government then, it will be very bad.

For Nangula, too, independence is 'the only hope one has. And of course it's a challenging thing, because one can only hope that it brings peace with justice. It will probably ask a lot of work from us, but I'm sure we are prepared to go for it.' Stressing the need to heal divisions caused by the war, she said 'Whatever reconciliation takes – I mean true reconciliation – we want to go for it'.

The only hope for women in Namibia has been independence, and now this has been achieved there is a chance for changes in women's situation.

# Postscript

'Discrimination against women is unconstitutional', proclaimed a banner carried by women in Namibia's independence parade on 21 March 1990. The marchers were giving a timely warning that the needs of women must not be ignored in the new Namibia.

Namibia has become independent under a new government since this book went to press. Elections in early November 1989 brought SWAPO to power, with 57 per cent of the vote, the DTA coming second with 28.5 per cent. Although SWAPO lacked a two-thirds majority (which would have enabled them to act without consulting the opposition), the constitution of the new Namibia was agreed – unanimously – within months. On 21 March 1990, Namibia's government, under President Sam Nujoma, was sworn in by the Secretary-General of the United Nations; the South African flag was lowered over Windhoek stadium, and the colours of the new nation were raised for the first time as independence was achieved.

While independence is the end of the long fight for freedom from colonial government, it is also, more importantly, only the beginning of the struggle for development. The conditions described in this book cannot be remedied overnight; neither can the inequalities of land distribution and wealth, particularly in view of the current anti-socialist world climate. There are, moreover, still political issues outstanding, principally that of Walvis Bay, which remains under South African occupation and should be returned to Namibia (as confirmed by UN Security Council Resolution 432 of 1978).

How will the policies and developments of the coming years fulfil the needs of Namibians, particularly women? Political representation of women is poor: only five of the 72 members of the Assembly are female, and only one of them, Libertine Amathila, is a minister. The constitution, however, makes specific provisions that will benefit women as black people, as women and as workers. It declares that 'no person shall be discriminated against on the grounds of sex, race, colour, ethnic origin, religion, creed, or social or economic status'. On racism it is particularly strong, holding 'the practice of racial discrimination and the practice and ideology of apartheid' to be criminal offences, 'for the purposes of expressing the revulsion of the Namibian people to such practices'.

Positive discrimination in favour of those previously disadvantaged is specifically permitted. In this context,

> it shall be permissible to have regard to the fact that women in Namibia have traditionally suffered special discrimination and that they need to be encouraged and enabled to play a full, equal and effective role in the political, social, economic and cultural life of the nation.

This is elaborated further on:

> The State shall actively promote and maintain the welfare of the people by adopting . . . policies aimed at the following: a) the enactment of legislation to ensure equality of opportunity for women, to enable them to participate fully in all spheres of Namibian society. In particular, the Government shall ensure the implementation of the principle of non-discrimination in remuneration of men and women. Further, the Government shall seek, through appropriate legislation, to provide maternity and related benefits for women.

This section goes on to commit the State to other policies, including the promotion of workers' rights.

The constitution also guarantees protection to the family as 'the natural and fundamental group unit of society'. While it is possible to see this as potentially repressive to women, we believe, on the contrary, that these provisions represent resistance to the onslaught made on the black family under colonialism, something of which we have tried to convey in this book. This onslaught has, of course, been highly detrimental to women's interests.[1]

The constitution will remain little more than a piece of paper until further legislation and, above all, action is undertaken. But Namibian women are keen to ensure that this happens. In the past they have fought for their freedom both as black people and as women. Whether they have engaged in active political work, or have been in the forefront of the struggle for survival, Namibian women will rise to the challenge of independence.

# Notes and References

## Chapter 1

1. Ndalikokule, J. in IDAF/AAM, October 1988.
2. Edwards, E. quoted in IDAF, 1988, p. 72.
3. Haitengela E. quoted in IDAF/AAM, 1988.
4. Personal interview with author, June 1988, at the time of the school's boycott.
5. McFadden, P. in B. Wood (ed.) 1988, p. 625.
6. Nambinga, R. M. quoted in IDAF 1988, p. 64.
7. Gawanas, B. in NSC, AON (Action on Namibia), London, Autumn 1988.
8. SWAPO, op. cit., p. 287.
9. *The Namibian*, 19 June 1988.
10. DTA: Democratic Turnhalle Alliance.
11. COSAWR (Committee on South African War Resistance) in B. Wood (ed.) 1988, p. 519.
12. Ibid.
13. MPLA: Popular Movement for the Liberation of Angola.
14. UNITA: National Union for the Total Independence of Angola.
15. IDAF 1989, p. 69.
16. Quoted in COSAWR, in B. Wood (ed.), 1988 p. 527.
17. *South* 11 June 1987, quoted in IDAF/AAM, 1988, op. cit.
18. COSAWR, in B. Wood (ed.) 1988, p. 528.
19. CIMS (Churches' Information and Monitoring Service) quoted in INON (International Newsbriefing on Namibia), No. 71, July/August 1989.
20. Ibid.
21. NCC (Namibia Communication Centre), quoted in Church Action on Namibia, *Rapid Response*, 8 September 1989.
22. Quoted by COSAWR, in B. Wood (ed.) 1988, p. 535.
23. Ipumbe, P. evidence given in the trial of Philip Wilkinson, in Conscientious Objector; The Trial. South African Bishop's Conference/End Conscription Campaign, Durban.
24. IDAF, 1989, op. cit., p. 29.
25. Personal interview with author, Windhoek, 1989.
26. Quoted in COSAWR, in B. Wood, (ed.) 1988, p. 533.
27. SWAPO, 1981, p. 178.
28. Quoted in IDAF, 198? p. 88.
29. SWAPO, 1981, p. 289.

## Chapter 2

1. First, R. in B. Wood (ed.) 1988, p. 326.
2. Allison, C. in B. Wood (ed.) 1988, p. 358.
3. Murray-Hudson, A. in B. Wood, 1988, p. 617
4. SWSC, in B. Wood (ed.) 1988, p. 353.
5. Moorsom, R. 1984b, p. 42.
6. Ndadi, V. 1989, pp. 60–77.
7. On women's employment in general, see Kazombaue, L. and Elago, N., in Tötemeyer, Kandetu and Werner (eds), 1987, pp. 198–201.
8. *Windhoek Observer*, 18 October 1986.
9. Uulenga, B. in Tötemeyer et al, 1987, pp. 119–20.
10. Quoted in Smith, S. 1986, p. 32.
11. Quoted in Cronje, G. and S. 1979, p. 61.
12. Kazombaue and Elago, 1987, p. 200.
13. Quoted in Cronje, G. and S., 1979, p. 61.
14. Uulenga, B. 1987, p. 121.
15. Cronje, G. and S. 1979, p. 61.
16. Murray-Hudson, A. op. cit., p. 618.
17. Ibid; Allison, C., op. cit., p. 360.
18. Allison, C., op. cit., pp. 360–1.
19. Von Garnier, C., (ed.) 1986.
20. Smith, S., 1986, p. 29.
21. Von Garnier, C., 1986, p. 2.
22. Quoted in Smith, S., 1986, p. 31.
23. IDAF, 1988, p. 32.
24. Smith, S., 1986, p. 34.
25. Ibid.
26. SWSC, 1988, pp. 354–5.
27. Moorsom, R., 1984, p. 37.
28. Quoted in Cronje, G. and S., 1979, p. 37.
29. Personal interview with author, Kavango, 1989.
30. Quoted in Smith, S., 1986, p. 28.
31. Von Garnier, C., 1986, pp. 2–3.
32. Smith S., 1986, pp. 32–3.
33. Ibid., p. 31; Von Garnier, C., 1986. p. 8.
34. Personal interview with author, Windhoek, 1989.
35. Moorehead, C., 1984, p. 27.

## Chapter 3

1. SWSC, in B. Wood (ed.) 1988.
2. Quotes from Sena Rautenbach, Cecilia Paulus and Loide Kassingo are from personal interview with author, Windhoek, 1989.
3. IDAF, 1988, p. 36.
4. Katjavivi, P. et. al., 1988, pp. 41–6; Ndadi, V., 1989.
5. Katjavivi, P. et al., 1988, p. 22.
6. Quoted in Cronje, G. and S., 1979, pp. 77–8.
7. Ibid., p. 103.

8. Ibid., pp. 79–87; IDAF, 1988, p. 36.
9. See especially SWAPO, 1981, pp. 226–7.
10. Cronje, G. and S., 1979, pp. 74, 76.
11. SWAPO, 1981, p. 268.
12. Moorsom, R., 1984, p. 42.
13. Cronje, G. and S., 1979, p. 105.
14. Ibid., p. 75–6.
15. SWAPO, 1981, p. 269.
16. Cronje, G. and S., 1979, p. 76.
17. IDAF, 1988, p. 37.
18. *AON*, summer 1988, p. 13.
19. *INON*, February and March, 1989, Nos. 66, 67.
20. Personal interview with author, Windhoek, August 1989.
21. *INON*, August 1988 and January 1989, Nos. 61, 65.
22. *AON*, summer 1988, p. 13; IDAF, 1988, p. 37.
23. *INON*, November 1987, March and April 1988, Nos. 53, 56, 57.

## Chapter 4

1. *The Namibian*, 25 March 1988.
2. IDAF, 1989, p. 65.
3. Haikali, E. in IDAF/AAM 1988.
4. UNIN, 1984, p. 20; IDAF, 1985, p. 3.
5. Hughson H., 1986, quoted in C. Moorehead 1988, p. 16.
6. UNIN, 1984, p. 21.
7. Smith S. 1986, pp. 31, 54.
8. UNIN, 1984, p. 25.
9. Abrahams, K. Interview quoted in C. Von Garnier, 1986, p. 53.
10. Ibid.
11. NSC Health Collective and T. Lobstein, 1984, p. 11.
12. Moorehead C., 1988, p. 23.
13. *The Namibian* 3 October 1986, quoted in IDAF/AAM, 1988.
14. IDAF, 1989, p. 42.
15. Moorehead, C., 1988, p. 28.
16. Ibid., p. 33.
17. Ibid., p. 25.
18. Poewe K., 1985, quoted in C. Von Garnier 1986, p. 53.
19. Smith S., 1986, p. 59.
20. *The Namibian* 6 June 1986, quoted in IDAF/AAM, 1988.
21. Von Garnier C., 1986, p. 54.
22. *The Namibian*, 9 October 1987, quoted in IDAF p. 75.
23. Lindsay J., 1987, quoted in IDAF/AAM, 1988.
24. Moorehead C., 1988, p. 18.
25. Indongo I., in Lobstein T. and NSC Health Collective, 1984 p. ix.

## Chapter 5

1. *INON*, May 1988, No. 58.

2. *INON*, July 1988, No. 60.
3. Moorehead, C., 1988, p. 12.
4. *INON*, August 1988, No. 61.
5. The head of the bantustan Owambo Administration. See appendix.
6. *INON*, August 1988, No. 61.
7. *INON*, September 1988, No. 62.
8. *INON*, October 1988, No. 63.
9. *The Namibian*, 24 February 1989.
10. See, for example, Wilfried Brock, in *AON*, autumn 1987, p. 6.
11. Haitengela, E., quoted in IDAF/AAM, 1988.
12. Smith, S., 1986, pp. 50–51.
13. IDAF, 1988, p. 48.
14. Ndilula, N., in B. Wood (ed.) 1988, p. 388.
15. IDAF, 1988, p. 49.
16. Moorehead, C., 1988, p. 10.
17. IDAF, 1988, p. 49.
18. Ellis, J., 1984, pp. 23, 25.
19. Ibid., p. 25.
20. IDAF, 1988, p. 50.
21. *The Namibian*, 24 February 1989.
22. English is seen as the language of liberation, because it makes possible study abroad and SWAPO has chosen it as the official language of Namibia after independence.
23. Brock, op. cit., 1987, pp. 6–7.
24. *INON*, August 1988, No. 61.
25. Ibid.
26. IDAF, 1988, p. 50.
27. Ellis, J., 1984, p. 25.
28. The school at Odibo was in fact moved south, to Onekwaya, after its position, one kilometre from the Angolan border, had made it the target of attacks in the 1970s.
29. The school is named after the Council of Churches in Namibia, from which it gets the funding for teachers' salaries, and is popularly called simply CCN.
30. Moorehead, C., 1988, p. 14.
31. A leader of the early white settlers.
32. SWAPO is a legal organization in Namibia (and was at the time of this interview) and it is lawful to belong to it. This has not prevented SWAPO members experiencing harassment.
33. *The Namibian*, 13 and 20 January 1989.
34. Chase, N., in Tötemeyer et. al., 1987, p. 149. In this context 'multiracial education' means the educating black children from different ethnic groups together, as opposed to state policy of keeping them separated.
35. Moorehead, C., 1988, p. 14.
36. Ibid., p. 14.
37. Smith, S., 1986, pp. 48, 51.
38. Ibid., p. 51.
39. Author's personal interview with literacy group participants, Kavango, 1989.

## Chapter 6

1. Moorsom, R., Transforming a Wasted Land; CIIR series, A Future for Namibia. 2: Agriculture. London 1982, p. 19.
2. SWC, in B. Wood (ed.) 1988, p. 347.
3. Kisiedu C.O., 1981.
4. SWSC/NSC, 1984.
5. Quoted in SWAPO, 1981, p. 285.
6. Nghidinwa, S., 1982.
7. McFadden, P., in B. Wood (ed.) 1988, p. 623.
8. SWAPO publication, Namibian Women in the Struggle.
9. Quoted in SWAPO 1981, p. 287.
10. SWC, 1987.
11. SWAPO, 1981, p. 291.
12. IDAF, 1989, p. 61.
13. SWC, 1987.
14. Ibid.
15. Quoted in SWAPO, 1981, p. 291.
16. Nghidinwa, S., 1982.
17. SWAPO, 1989, p. 19.
18. SWC, in B. Wood (ed.) 1988, p. 355.

## Chapter 7

1. Strauss, A., in C. Von Garnier (ed.) 1986, p. 184.
2. Amutenya, W., in Tötemeyer et. al., 1987, p. 217.
3. UN, 1985.
4. Strauss, A., in C. Von Garnier (ed.) 1986, p. 191.
5. This interview was held in late May 1988.
6. Etango and Ezuva: state-run 'cultural'/political organizations.
7. UN, 1985.

## Chapter 8

1. WCC PCR, 'The Way to Namibian Indepedence: UN Resolution 435', p. 14.
2. Soggot, D. 1986, p. 13.
3. Ibid.
4. Hunke, H., in B. Wood (ed.) 1988, p. 629–30.
5. Ibid., p. 629.
6. WCC PCR, op cit, p. 14.
7. Soggot, D., 1986, p. 15.
8. Hunke, H., on B. Wood (ed.) 1988, p .629.
9. WCC PCR, op cit, p. 14.
10. SWAPO, 1981, pp. 168–9.
11. AMEC, in particular is, however, still very active, and is the support network behind the highly successful independent school at Gibeon.
12. SWAPO, 1981, p. 169.
13. See p. 65.

14. Soggott, D., 1986, pp. 35–7.
15. Auala, Gowaseb and Winter, in B. Wood (ed.) 1988, pp. 638–9.
16. NCC press release, 21 January 1987.
17. Willy Amutenya, in Tötemeyer, et. al., 1987, p. 216.
18. /Ai-//Gams is the pre-colonial name for Windhoek, and means 'hot springs'.
19. Zephaniah Kameeta, in Tötemeyer et. al., 1987, pp. 209–12.
20. WCC PCR, op cit, p. 15.
21. Author's interview with Nangula Kathindi, Windhoek, 1989.
22. Quoted in Kameeta, Z., in Tötemeyer et. al., 1987, pp. 207–8.
23. Hunke, H., in B. Wood (ed.) 1988, pp. 630–2.
24. Personal interview with author, Kavango, 1989.
25. *Windhoek Advertiser*, 5 June 1989.

## Postscript

1. See the *Constition of the Republic of Namibia*, articles 10 (2); 23; 95 (1); 14.

# Bibliography

African–European Institute, The Hague (1989) 'Namibia: The Last Steps to Genuine Independence?' Conference Document, Harare 3–4 April.

Allison, C. (1986) *It's Like Holding the Key to Your Own Jail*, World Council of Churches, Geneva.

Cronje, G. & S. (1979) *The Workers of Namibia*, IDAF, London.

Ellis, J. (1984) *Education, Repression and Liberation: Namibia*, CIIR and World University Service, London.

Herbstein, D. and Evenson, J. (1989) *The Devils are Among Us: The War for Namibia*, Zed Books, London.

Hishongwa, N. D. (1983) *Women of Namibia*, Bg and Bygd, Vimmerby.

IDAF, (1985) 'A Nation in Peril: Health in Apartheid Namibia' (Fact Paper on Southern Africa No. 13), London.

——— (1989) *Namibia: The Facts*, London.

IDAF/AAM, (1988) *Children, Apartheid and Repression*. Papers presented at London Conference, October.

Katjavivi, P. (1988) *A History of Resistance in Namibia*, James Currey, London.

——— Frostin, P. and Mbuende, K. (1989) *Church and Liberation in Namibia*, Pluto Press, London.

Kisiedu, C. O. (1981) *The Situation of Women Living under Racist Regimes*, UN Institute for Namibia, Lusaka.

Lobstein, T. and NSC Health Collective (1984) *Namibia: Reclaiming the People's Health*, AON Publications, London.

Moorehead, C. (1988) *Namibia, Apartheid's Forgotten Children*, OXFAM, Oxford.

Moorsom, R. (1982) *Agriculture: Transforming a Wasted Land*, CIIR, London.

——— (1984a) *Fishing: Exploiting the Sea*, CIIR, London.

——— (1984b) *Walvis Bay: Namibia's Port*, IDAF, London.

Ndadi, V. (1989) *Breaking Contract*, IDAF, London.

Nghidinwa, S. (1982). SWAPO and the Machineries for the Integration of Namibian Women in Development. Paper presented at the Regional Seminar on Machineries for the Integration of Women in Development in Africa, Addis Ababa, November.

Smith, S. (1986) *Namibia – A Violation of Trust*, OXFAM, Oxford.

Soggot, D. (1986) *Namibia: The Violent Heritage*, Rex Collings, London.

South African Bishops' Conference/End Conscription Campaign, *Conscientious Objector: The Trial*, Durban.

SWAPO, (1989) *SWAPO's Election Manifesto*, Windhoek.

——— (1981) *To Be Born a Nation*, Zed Press, London.

SWC, (1987) 'The Situation and Conditions of Women and Children under Apartheid Colonialism in Namibia', paper presented on a speaking tour to the USA.

SWSC/NSC, (1984) 'Class, Gender and Race', paper presented to the International Conference on Namibia, City University, London.

Tötemeyer, G., V. Kandetu and W. Werner (eds), (1987) *Namibia in Perspective*, Council of Churches in Namibia.

UNIN, (1984) *Health Sector Policy Options for Independent Namibia.*

Von Garnier, C. (ed.) (1986) *Katutura Revisited*, Windhoek.

Wood, B. (ed.) (1988) *Readings on Namibia's History and Society 1884–1984*, NSC/UNIN, London.

———/NCC, (1989) *The UN Plan for Namibia and its Initial Implementation*, London.

World Conference to Review and Appraise the Achievements of the UN Decade for Women, (1985) *Report*, Nairobi.

WCC PCR, (1988) *The Way to Namibian Independence: UN Resolution 435*, Geneva.

## Periodicals

NSC, *International News Briefing on Namibia* (INON)
NSC, *Action on Namibia* (AON)
CAN, *Newsletter*
The *Namibian* newspaper

## Useful Organizations

Anti-Apartheid Movement (AAM)
13 Mandela Street, London NW1 0DW. Tel: 071-387 7966

British Defence and Aid Fund for Southern Africa (BDAF)
Unit 22, The Ivories, 6–8 Northampton Street, London N1 2HX. Tel: 071-359 7729

Church Action on Namibia (CAN)
Praxis, URC Church, Pott Street, London E2 0EF. Tel: 071-729 7985

End Loans to South Africa (ELTSA)
c/o Methodist Church, 56 Camberwell Road, London, SE5 0EN. Tel: 071-708 4702

International Defence and Aid Fund for Southern Africa (IDAF)
64 Essex Road, London, N1 8LR. Tel: 071-359 9181

Namibia Communications Centre (NCC)
PO Box 286, London WC1X 0EL. Tel: 071-833 2905

Namibia Support Committee (NSC)
PO Box 16, London, NW5 2LW

SWAPO of Namibia
PO Box 194, London, N5 1LW. Tel: 071-359 9116

# Index

**Zed Books Ltd**

is a publisher whose international and Third World lists span:

- **Women's Studies**
- **Development**
- **Environment**
- **Current Affairs**
- **International Relations**
- **Children's Studies**
- **Labour Studies**
- **Cultural Studies**
- **Human Rights**
- **Indigenous Peoples**
- **Health**

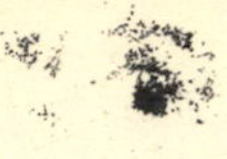

We also specialize in Area Studies where we have extensive lists in African Studies, Asian Studies, Caribbean and Latin American Studies, Middle East Studies, and Pacific Studies.

For further information about books available from Zed Books, please write to: Catalogue Enquiries, Zed Books Ltd, 57 Caledonian Road, London N1 9BU. Our books are available from distributors in many countries (for full details, see our catalogues), including:

**In the USA**

Humanities Press International, Inc., 171 First Avenue,
Atlantic Highlands, New Jersey 07716.
Tel: (201) 872 1441;
Fax: (201) 872 0717.

**In Canada**

DEC, 229 College Street, Toronto, Ontario M5T 1R4.
Tel: (416) 971 7051.

**In Australia**

Wild and Woolley Ltd, 16 Darghan Street, Glebe, NSW 2037.

**In India**

Bibliomania, C-236 Defence Colony, New Delhi 110 024.

**In Southern Africa**

David Philip Publisher (Pty) Ltd, PO Box 408, Claremont 7735,
South Africa.